# THE GRIEF HELPLINE

## Restoring Your Joy After Experiencing a Personal Loss

# PRAISE FOR THE GRIEF HELPLINE

## Endorsement

Vernessa's story is deeply moving, and those who have suffered great loss in their life will be able to relate to her struggles. Vernessa is an overcomer. She has discovered how to live more honestly and authentically because of her journey through grief. Like the mythological phoenix that rose from the ashes a new creature, Vernessa has, through her faith, moved from her life of trials into a bold witness to God's ability to transform her life and yours.

Her story of survival is inspirational, and she has now taken what was once painful to her and turned it into this book to benefit others. Her message combined with the timing of this book is perfection.

You will find this book is divided into two sections: Grief Recovery and Joy Restoration. You can work through them in any order that feels natural for you, based on where you're at.

As you meditate through the sections dedicated to thought, word, prayer, and challenge, your life will begin to change. Allow God to speak to you in those times. God is there in that quiet place, just waiting for you to show up.

Congratulations, Vernessa, on your book. You are an amazing woman!

**Leelo Bush, PhD**
"America's Doctor of Joy"
CEO / Founder of the Professional Christian Coaching
 & Counseling Academy
www.pccca.org


A few months ago, I lost someone extremely close to me, and I became absolutely devastated. I fell into a deep depression and couldn't even get out of bed on some mornings. Not surprisingly, both my personal life and my professional life began to suffer. But based off of a recommendation from a trusted friend, I decided to try Vernessa's Grief Helpline services. I was all but hopeless in my life, but while attending her Joy Restoration Retreat, I began to think more positively. What made it such a great experience is that Vernessa worked with me one-on-one and created a personalized approach in which I started to make changes in my life immediately through setting short-term and long-term goals. The fact that Vernessa has suffered through so much grief in her own life means that she speaks from experience. I'm happy to say that I've turned my life around in many ways and have been able to move forward in a positive manner. Highly recommended!

**Teressa Sommers**


After my wife passed away, I no longer knew what to do with myself. She had been a part of my life for over 20 years, and losing her meant that I was no longer whole. Being raised in a way that meant that expressing my feelings as a man was not acceptable, I didn't open up to anyone. Enter Grief Helpline. I saw an advertisement for it and figu ed that I really did want to pour out my feelings to someone who wouldn't judge me. On a whim, I joined a Vision Board Party and Retreat that Vernessa offered and felt that I made the right decision as soon as I met her. I had lost my zeal for life and the ambition that once defined me, and this retreat helped me get it all back. Vernessa helped me to reignite my own life goals and, most importantly, got me to dream big again! Her coaching through the Grief Helpline was invaluable and is a service that I would strongly suggest for anyone who is going through some tough personal times.

**Larry Myers**

**THE GRIEF HELPLINE**

Published by Purposely Created Publishing Group™

Copyright © 2017 Vernessa Blackwell

ALL RIGHTS RESERVED.

Printed in the United States of America

ISBN (ebook): 978-1-945558-08-5
ISBN (paperback): 978-1-945558-07-8

Special discounts are available on bulk quantity purchases by book clubs, associations and special interest groups. For details email: sales@publishyourgift.com or call (888) 949-6228.

*For information logon to:*
www.PublishYourGift.com

*Now to Him who is able to [carry out His purpose and] do superabundantly more than all that we dare ask or think [infini ely beyond our greatest prayers, hopes, or dreams], according to His power that is at work within us, to Him be the glory in the church and in Christ Jesus throughout all generations forever and ever. Amen.*

Ephesians 3:20–21 Amplified Bibl

# DEDICATION

First, I'd like to give honor to my Lord and Savior, who is the head of my life.

Second, I wish to acknowledge my mom, my dad, and all my siblings: Hazel, Cheetah, Gary, and Alicia. Not a day goes by that I don't think of you. I miss you all so much.

Third, I wouldn't be myself if I failed to mention the love of my life, my heartbeat, Paul. I'll forever miss you.

I think about the good times all of us shared. We laughed together and cried together. I feel so alone since you all are gone, but I know that one day I'll see you all again. I pray your souls are resting in peace.

I'd also like to honor my daughters, Darkema and Takia. You have inspired me to move forward in writing the next chapter of my life and start my coaching businesses: Moving from Grief to Joy.

My goal is to leave a legacy for my daughters and my wonderful grandchildren: Tyquan, Kemonte, Khyeema, Davonte, Khalil, Terrence, and Kamille. I love all of you with my whole heart.

This book is a tribute to all of my loved ones who have passed on before me.

# TABLE OF CONTENTS

# FOREWORD

Grief is a serious emotion! Though it's a normal part of life if not handled properly, it can steal our joy, causing long-term mental suffering, physical illness, and can even shorten life. The scriptures say that joy comes from God to provide us with strength. Grief is the opposite of joy. Whether its affliction, regret, loss, or even being deeply affected by the cares of the world, if it's giving you a heavy heart or an undercurrent of unshakable sorrow, it's not to be taken lightly. Without a heart-centered coach or counselor who specializes in grief, you can end up living under a spirit of oppression without ever knowing why. This is why so many people feel disempowered and emotionally challenged. What's worst is when they go to their doctor for help and end up on debilitating sleep aids, anxiety medication, and psychotropic drugs. This road leads down a slippery slope that steals the quality of life of thousands every day, all because of unsettled sorrow.

Then there are the suppressers. These folks can shake off every blow that life hits them with (so they think). Unfortunately, from that first untreated emotional blow, a wound is developed. It's only a matter of time after continuous unresolved emotional hits that one day, in some way, that festering wound will surface from the subconscious, open, and release. I call that a "cocoon experience."

I was more of the suppressed type rather than the oppressed type. After 15 years in the wellness field, in 2007, I had my "cocoon experience" where everything began to fall apart at the same time, including my marriage, finances, business, and health. I boldly asked God to not only free me from the horrifying blood disease, but also to heal my mind, emotions, marriage, and finances. He began to reveal to me how my downward spiral was the result of the emotional mess and mayhem that I had allowed to build up in my mind and emotions. In other words, this "faith-filled" woman of God had a toxic soul. It all began to make sense, the passing of my 41-year-old mom, followed by my 54-year-old dad, then having my only brother's life cut short at 37, while my sister was dealing with a serious health crisis. Not long after my brother died, seven other close relatives passed on in less than two years. Never once did I speak to a coach or counselor for grief.

How different would things have been had I read Vernessa Blackwell's book, The Grief Helpline, years ago? How grateful am I to have it today? Very! Not only is she a certified grief and joy restoration coach, Vernessa is the only person I know who has had to face the death of a loved one as many times as I have. She has the gift to guide you through the healing process with the love and understanding that can only come from someone who's been there.

Until you're ready to hire Vernessa to help you get your joy back, read her book The Grief Helpline. It is a must-read for everyone! Whether you're experiencing grief for the first time or you have a lifetime of regrets and losses, you need help in order to heal.

Carmen Abercrombie aka Coach Carmen
Holistic Health, Purpose & Wealth Coach
www.SharingTheBliss.com

# INTRODUCTION
## MY STORY

Some mornings, I wake up and can barely believe the people I love are now gone to a place unknown to me. Within a five and a half year period, beginning when I was 23, I lost six family members. Death started to become almost too familiar. The pain came and went in waves and could never be predicted.

My losses began in the spring of 1982, while I was finishing basic training and going through Advanced Individual Training in the army. One of my favorite cousins, who was only thirteen, was murdered. There was a boy who liked her and wanted to talk to her, so he asked her to come out and play. She told him she was teaching her friends a new dance and would see him later. He got upset, ran into her mother's kitchen, grabbed a knife from the cabinet drawer, threw it, and it stuck in her heart. Though the incident occurred at her mother's house, she was actually raised by my grandma who lived directly across the street. After it had happened, she ran out of the front door and tried to make it back to her house. She collapsed in front of her home and died. I loved my cousin, and this was devastating for the entire family. She was only a child, but she had a very promising future as a dancer.

Then in 1984, the Easter holiday was approaching, and I had to make a decision as to where I would spend it. I decided to go see my parents. My mom said my dad wasn't feeling well. He had been looking and talking like he was out of his mind. My Mom said he had been like that for a day or so. He looked so weak and frail. This startled me. I imagined the worst and thought he did not have much time left. This disturbed me, so I called the paramedics to take him to the hospital. I could sense he didn't have much time left, so I went with him. I thought I might not get another chance. As we were en route to the hospital, I asked him if he was okay. He said, "Baby, the grass is so pretty and green on the other side of the fence." I was experiencing something I'd never been acquainted with before. I didn't even know the true extent of it yet. Daddy slipped into a coma and passed away a few days later.

I sat at the end of the table next to the phone when we received the call that he was gone. My mother was at the opposite end of the room, and my sister, Cheetah, sat next to me holding my hand, looking into my eyes. She had a reassuring look on her face. I couldn't look at them. I sat there in fear while tears streamed down my face. The pit of my stomach turned and filled with anxiety. All I could do was cry. It was as if my worst nightmare had come to life. The anxious feeling in the pit of my stomach made me uncomfortable everywhere. I tried laying down, but I couldn't get settled. I cried the entire day.

I felt sorry for my daughter, who sat next to me on the couch and questioned my distraught state. This was my first extensive experience with death. There were no words that would relieve my pain. My first thought was to close my eyes. I tried to sleep, but my body simply wouldn't allow me to. I thought in these moments that I would never rest again. I couldn't believe this was happening.

That night, I spent my first evening with family at my parents' house since my father's death. I carried my suitcase into the house and put it off to the side in the living room. I plopped down, undid the zippers, and began rummaging through my belongings. I did this to avoid my discomfort with everything that had taken place during the previous twenty-four hours.

The next day, we went to the funeral home. My mother was handling the arrangements. We cried. We fumed. We felt sad and angry. And we laughed. We stood outside the funeral home after the arrangements were made and laughed and joked about Daddy. Oh how he would be missed. We remembered the good times with the bad. We laughed while we cried. We all truly loved our father, each in our own way.

We decided to drive together to North Carolina where his funeral service would be held. My father loved fishing and his car. For years, Daddy drove us around in in his Chevrolet Impala that he had simply adored. Daddy always said that if he died, just take the old Chevy and push it into the sea. He was a true, diehard Chevrolet lover. What I had in mind was a little less dramatic! I suggested that we drive the old

Chevy to his funeral. Everyone agreed, and so we were off on a painful trip.

After his death, my mother was left to care for four children alone. She did an amazing job. My sister Cheetah was the oldest sister living nearby; Gary was next; I was after Gary; and Lish was the baby. My childhood flashed before my eyes. Times were great when Dad was here, but things got a little tough after that. For twenty-five years, I got to be Daddy's little girl, and I am so grateful for that time with him. I had the best father a girl could want. I know he would be proud of who I am today. I know he would have been upset by some of my choices in the past, but I also know he would still love me all the same.

A few months went by, and I felt like I was working through my grief. My impending divorce was sailing through the legal system, yet I was constantly overcome with heartache because of my loss. I started a new job. That's when I received a phone call from my mother. My life was turned upside down again—my uncle was in the hospital. We drove back to North Carolina to be with him in his final hours.

My grief process, once again, was reset to the beginning. Sorrow and grief consumed my life. I felt as though things would never return to normal. I couldn't even remember what that felt like. My brother, sisters, and I were experiencing fatigue, depression, sadness, and other assorted emotions. My sister Cheetah, however, seemed to have the most difficulty. She fell deeper and deeper into a depression.

One evening, approximately eight months after my father died, my sister called me at home. She said she needed to talk to me about something very important. I had no idea what she was going to tell me. She confessed that she was thinking about moving back to North Carolina to be with her kids. She wanted to retire and go back home, so she asked me to look after Mom. I couldn't believe what I was hearing, but I held my composure, letting tears stream down my cheeks, while I listened to her rationalize why she had decided to leave. Cheetah was my sounding board. She listened to me about everything and never criticized. I truly hated to see her go, but I realized it would be selfish to ask her to stay.

Once Cheetah moved, I started to look after Mama. Mama was a joy. She was loving and supportive, but she didn't take any stuff. I loved my mother, so I wanted to give back to her and help in any way, I took on a second job as a pizza delivery driver. Some days she would ride with me, and we would laugh and joke.

Six months later, I drove to North Carolina to see my cousin, Anthony, who we called "Boo." Again, I was on a dreaded mission. (I have experienced a lot of driving in the most unpleasant ways.) My cousin could barely speak or walk at this point. He relied on his mother for his everyday care. I saw on my cousin's face his desire to get out of bed. The next day, after his mother left, I decided to put him in his wheelchair and take him outside.

I pulled him up and sat him back against the bed to prop him up so that I could put his coat on. It was as if I was dressing a

21

lifeless child. He couldn't help me. I struggled and struggled, trying to move his arms about in a way that would enable me to slip the coat on. At some point during this process, we both began laughing uncontrollably at my sorry attempts to help.

After the jacket was on, the hard part came. I propped his weight on me and slowly walked him to the front lobby. Now take into consideration that we weren't the same height or weight, and all he was capable of was a slight shuffle. I managed to sit him down on the top step. I needed to rest a minute. And although I wasn't quite sure how I was going to get him down the stairs, I was so damned determined that he was going to get to spend some time outdoors to see and hear the birds he loved.

After resting for a moment, I got up behind him and slipped my arms underneath his arms. I pulled him up and sat him down on the next step; then I moved each leg down a step farther. Step by step, we slowly worked our way down those stairs, hoisting him with all my energy, not thinking about my body. I pulled him up and placed him into the wheelchair. Mission accomplished, or so I thought.

I wheeled him around the neighborhood. There was a chill in the air, but it was pleasant, and not too cold. The birds were chirping their lungs out. My cousin looked around taking everything in. I looked at his childlike face and was struck with so much pain that it felt like I had a knife stuck in my heart. He was failing.

It came time to take him back in, and I almost cried when I realized that I had to figure out a way to get him back up the stairs. So once again, I began. I placed him on the bottom step, got behind him, and pulled him up each step, putting each foot up a step each time as I moved him. After the long journey, we finally made it back into the house and took our coats off. I was amazed at how insane I could be at times. I knew I'd pay for it later that night.

I don't know if this was his last visit outside, but I'm grateful that I had the strength and tenacity to accomplish this adventure. I woke up that next morning in excruciating pain. Every muscle in my back and shoulders was sore. The grief I was feeling because of the deaths that had already occurred, and the fate of my cousin, left me feeling exhausted. It was a heart-wrenching experience. I wanted to do more but could not. I felt frustrated and helpless. I couldn't give up my job or take enough time off to stay with him until he passed. My life needed to function. I had bills to pay. And that pissed me off.

At that point, I really thought nothing else bad could happen. Then, I got word from my mother that my grandmother died. I loved my grandma. We had stayed with her during the summer on and off throughout my life. Even though I mourned her, I really mourned the loss of my complete family. I also mourned the opportunities that were now gone. No more family get togethers. No more chats with Grandma. No more memories.

A couple of weeks later, I took a second trip to see Anthony. This time, he was totally paralyzed and comatose. I had no idea if he understood that I was there or not. I have to believe he did. I didn't know what else I could do for him other than to be by his side, just simply being there.

I remember times going out, shopping at the mall, or the grocery store, and looking into the faces of other people. I wondered what was happening in their lives. I wondered if they had any clue about what I was going through. I wanted to tell everyone about my pain. I needed to share it, but the few I told didn't understand the depth of the pain and despair that I felt. I felt as though I needed to scream from the Empire State Building what had happened to me. I needed the world to embrace me and the adversities I endured.

Approximately fourteen years after my father's death, my mother passed away. My mother was a real fighter.

On February 27 1998, we discovered that my mother had cancer. I couldn't believe that after everything and everyone I'd already lost in my life that at the age of 35, I would be told my mom had *cancer*! Though it was somewhat shocking, I have to say that because I had been through so much, it didn't surprise me. It was almost as if I expected tragedy to happen. I was used to it. Through all of that, I learned how to live more honestly and real because of going through the grief, but now, with cancer, it put things into even more perspective. Traffic jams didn't seem such a big deal anymore, and everything was seeming pretty surreal.

The most frightening moment was when my mom had to have radiology to see if the tumor she had in her lung was malignant. After they had taken the x-ray, they asked my sister and I to wait a moment just to make sure they took clear pictures. It wasn't known by any of them that this is where the cancer was. After what seemed like an eternity but was actually only a few minutes, the technician came back into the room. They said that the radiologist wanted to take a look at her chest at a different angle. (It wasn't known by any of them that this was where the cancer was.) I started to panic and told the tech that, after the x-ray had been reviewed by the radiologist, I wanted to talk to them. I didn't want my mom to get the bad news by herself. I asked if they could give us a few days before they told her the results so I could notify other family members to be there when she received the bad news. In a split second, I knew that if this was cancer in my mother's lungs, she was as good as gone.

The x-rays showed that the tumor was enlarged and didn't look good for her at all.

In those few moments, from the time the tech took the second shot of my mother's chest to the time the radiologist came back in to consult with my sister and me, my life flashed before my eyes. I'd heard that expression before, but I never truly knew what it meant. There were a few minutes while waiting for the radiologist to talk to me that an indescribable panic came over me. Could this truly be it for Mama? I mean, why Mama?

The doctor wanted to take a biopsy and find out if Mama's tumor was benign or malignant. The procedure was painful, but again, my mother was a real fighter. I'll never forget the day she was diagnosed with that terrible disease. I walked upstairs and saw her peacefully sleeping on the adjustable hospital bed. I looked over at my sister, and the doctor told us the biopsy was malignant. I almost fell to my knees. I knew I couldn't collapse in front of her. I had to be strong for her, but it hit me just how incredibly young and unprepared I really was for life without my mama.

I knew I didn't want Mom to be alone, so I went home to call my family and loved ones who lived out of town. I told them the news and told them to hurry—she didn't have long. I wanted them to get to see Mama before she left us.

Mama passed away in March of 1998. It's been seventeen years since she left. No one has been able to make me laugh like Mama. No one has been able to make me as angry either. No one has been able to make me feel as safe or as loved. In that exact moment, I knew that chapter of my life was closed. I could never go home and just be a daughter. Her daughter. Then, in December of 1998, Paul's only daughter, Natosha, was killed. Her and her best friend, Melissa, were gunned down on the street in DC. Tosha was a beautiful girl; she was gifted and talented. She was a doll.

The all-too-familiar torment struck again when my sister Cheetah passed away in 2005. I loved my sister Cheetah. She was always considered the big sister. Sweet and loving, she led and paved the way for me. I received a lot of my mental toughness from her. I press on in her memory for I know she was an amazing person and gave up so much for her family.

In 2007, tragedy struck again. My love, my friend, my confidante, my lover, for over thirty years was killed in a car accident. I was blessed to have him for over thirty years. Paul was a great guy. He was fun loving, supportive, and full of joy. Paul was loved by all.

Two years later, my nephew Patrick passed away from stomach cancer. This was a hard one too. When he found out he had cancer, he called home to share the news. He was living in Indiana at the time. My aunt Annette, my brother Gary, and I took a road trip. The cancer was in the early stages then, or so we thought.

We talked about it, and he told me he was not ready to leave us. He was in his early forties. He said he still had a lot of stuff he wanted to do. I shared with him what God had dropped in my spirit to share: God has a plan for all of us. He still had time to make it right or get it right, to go to church, and continue to pray. To make sure he repented of his sins and ask God to save his soul. I also advised him that God was a healer. I told him we would be praying for him, so not to worry. I asked him to get the treatment and be kind to the doctors. They were sent to take care of him in his time of need. The cancer spread quickly, and within six to eight weeks, he passed away—too soon. Two days after my nephew's death, on May 23, 2009, my brother Gary passed away from a massive heart attack.

My Aunt called me two days after Patrick died. She asked if I was sitting down because she had something to tell me. I said yes. I'd just sat down on the edge of the bed and had begun taking my boots off. She said, "Gary had a massive heart attack, and he's passed away." I asked if she was serious;

she said he wasn't breathing when they left for the hospital. I told her that I had to call her back. I had to hang up and get myself together because, like I said, I had just talked to him the day before. On top of that, he didn't have any life insurance. So when they brought my nephew back from Milwaukee, I asked my family to merge the funerals because I couldn't handle two back-to-back like that. Plus, my oldest sister, Hazel, had emphysema and was in a wheelchair.

In 2012, my sister Hazel passed away. Hazel was one of a kind. God bless her soul. She always had a story to tell. I would sit and talk to Hazel and laugh for hours. She found humor in life. She stayed in Milwaukee most of my younger years and moved back to Maryland when Mom got sick. After Mama passed, Hazel decided to stay near family, so we did get close as sisters as adults even though she lived far away as a child. I thank God for the visits, the memories, and the love we shared as a whole. I think all my siblings live on in me. I know they live in my heart, for I truly miss them and think of them often.

The most recent test of my faith was in December of 2014. Alicia, "Lish," my baby sister, passed away. This hit me hard, like a ton of bricks had landed on my chest. Her daughter left my brother-in-law and I responsible for cleaning out her apartment. This was devastating. She had all these pictures of us when we were young. There were so many memories right there in her apartment. Lish was a pack rat and didn't throw anything away. There were obituaries and memorial programs—it was a map through our past. She was three years younger than me, so she and I were very close. I was crushed. It was at this moment that I realized I had to do something to help others get through times like these.

My entire family died at young ages: Cheetah at 53, Lish at 52, Gary at 54, and Hazel at 69. I thought, was God trying to tell me something? I had gone through too much and had too much to share with others to let this experience just be in vain. All I have left are my children, nieces, nephews, grandchildren, and one loving auntie on my mom's side, Aunt Annette. Thank God for my aunts and uncles on my dad's side. I still have quite a few: Aunt Bessie, Aunt Jean, Aunt Elaine, Aunt Dorothy, and Uncle David. However, I have hope for a bright future. Memories of my family will never fade. The lessons keep on coming. As the saying goes, God doesn't give us anything we cannot handle.

So here I am now, the sole survivor, and still very inspired, with a positive attitude. Life is unfolding in its divine manner, and though I don't always understand why these tragedies happen, life always works itself out. I do the most I can to turn my painful situations and experiences into something that benefit others. Even though tragedy has befallen me multiple times, I'm still happy. This is because my faith is rock solid. I know God works through me to help guide others.

Until the day my brother Gary died, through all the pain and suffering he had to endure, he continued to joke and have a positive attitude. I watched and learned from my brother, who had an incredibly infectious and positive attitude. I knew that this was how I wanted to handle tragedies and adversity in my life.

Because of affliction, you feel helpless. It seems as though someone is causing these things to happen to you. You might even think God is causing these bad things to happen to you. But it isn't true. If you wish to truly be a strong person, you must understand that you're not being afflicted by God or anyone else. You're being afflicted by the things that happened to you. There's a huge difference between being afflicted by people and circumstances. You cannot blame anyone.

My faith tells me that God is here to help me through tragedy. Even though these tragedies occurred and affected me, they strengthened my faith. I know this to be true for you, too. My experiences are a gift from God. They are lessons that have empowered me to write a book about how I've persevered through hardships.

Because of my faith, I've remained resilient. You can too. You can make a difference in the lives of others, like I hope to. Grief has a purpose. I live, laugh, and love incessantly because of it. Yes, life is short. You may get knocked down, but you're not out. You are not out of the fight. Get back up. You're in this thing to win it. Remember, it's a matter of choice, and it's up to you in how you let your life's events affect your life. May your path be strong and may God grant you the will to move from grief to joy.

. . .

In between the tragedies, I tried to move on in my life, over and over again. Once upon a time, there were five of us. Now I'm the only one left. For a while, I dealt with my grief by keeping

place that we used to go together, I get emotional. I often find myself looking at my phone and knowing that it's not going to ring. It was even hard visiting the nail shop we frequented together because the technicians would ask where she was, and I'd share that she passed away. Then there's the, "I'm so sorry to hear that." It's tough.

Holidays and special dates that meant something to you and that person are no more. You have to face them alone now. Mother's Day, for example, is really hard for someone who's lost their mom, especially if they had a close relationship. Then, there are birthdays. You think about it the day before, or even the week before. You think about how Mom's birthday would have been August.3. You think about it the whole month, and when the date finally hits, you think about it even more. "Happy birthday, Mom. I know you're not here, but I still love you and think about you." When you have someone else close by to celebrate in honor of that person's memory, then it's a lot easier. But if your family lives far away or you're deployed like I was, and have no one but you, you deal with it by yourself. You have to have something to help you and give you the courage to get through it.

This devotional is that something. It was designed for you. In it, I share my story and my process as a means of supporting you through your journey of healing. I understand that people grieve differently. Therefore, there's no guide or self-help book that can teach you how to move on with your life. That's not what I intend to do. Instead, this book will show you how to transform your perspective and thought process into one that allows you to heal at your own pace while encouraging productivity (not busyness, as there is a difference), passion, and purpose.

God doesn't make mistakes. We were born, and we know we have to leave here eventually. Acknowledging that small fact helped me to get my life back in order because I was just living for myself and my kids, but I soon realized that it's not about me. It's about what God called me here to do. So perform the mission that He sent you here to do. Starting my business was the first step in deciding that it was time to find out what my purpose was. After that, there was no stopping me. I had concerns along the way, but I had to walk it out. Don't worry about how you're going to do it because He's going to make a way. He always does.

# How to Use This Book

This book is divided into two sections: Grief Recovery and Joy Restoration. You're not required to read this book from beginning to end. Perhaps you'd like to read from the section that calls to your spirit for that day. If you're feeling particularly sorrowful, maybe you'd like to go straight to the Grief Recovery section. Or, if you're like me, then maybe you'd like to flip to a random page and see what message finds you.

Each day is composed of a thought, word, prayer, and challenge. The daily thought is a simple reflection or story of mine that I share to give you background on the upcoming word, prayer, and challenge. The word is a scripture that can be found in the Bible to give you spiritual support for that day. The prayer, like the word, is also designed for spiritual support. Feel free, however, to pray your own prayer. Finally, the challenge is a prompt that moves the advice from something that you read to something that you do. It isn't until we implement the practices in our lives that we actually experience a difference.

Some challenges require writing. For these, you'll need a pen and a notebook. I recommend the *Journey to Joy Journal* for your work with this book. Don't combine this book with recipes, to-do lists, or anything else. It'll detract from helping you. While the prompts may give you a certain time or set of questions, don't feel limited to them. This is your journey and your devotional; treat it as such. Think of your writing exercises as your time to speak with God.

In addition to speaking with God, we'll also be reserving time to listen. These are in the form of meditations. The purpose of meditation is to silence your busy, distracting thoughts. You're mentally and physically giving yourself a much-needed timeout. If you aren't already familiar, here's a basic guide to do so:

Sit comfortably in a quiet place.

Close your eyes or find a focal point, and breathe in through your nose.

As you exhale, silently repeat your mantra or affirmation to yourself.

Aim to spend at least ten minutes meditating.

Enjoy.

# Part I: Grief Recovery

# Part I: Grief Recovery

*"For everything there is a season, and a time for every matter under heaven: a time to be born, and a time to die; a time to plant, and a time to pluck up what is planted; a time to kill, and a time to heal; a time to break down, and a time to build up; a time to weep, and a time to laugh; a time to mourn, and a time to dance; a time to cast away stones, and a time to gather stones together."* Ecclesiastes 3:1-5 ESV

Sadness and sorrow are part of the human experience. Many times, souls will do anything to avoid it by keeping busy or taking a trip, and ignoring their emotions. When sorrow comes, it must be accepted. It's part of your worldly experience as a soul. It cannot be avoided or wished away. Sorrow must be felt and honored for the gift that it is. The place of sorrow is the place of growth and new beginnings. During times of sorrow, you have the potential for unlimited life changes and transformation. But in order for transformation to happen, the sorrow must be faced directly and deeply to the very core of your pain. It must be experienced as is, without anger, blame, or victimhood.

People would say to me, "Oh, I know how you feel," and I'd think, "You don't know how I feel right now. Maybe you've been through this, but how long ago was it? And if you do know how I feel, what did you do to make yourself feel better?"

When my mom passed away in 1998, I sought out counseling. In addition to the counseling, my sisters, my brother, and I started to bond more and bring the kids around each other in an effort to get through it together. As my siblings started passing away, it was just me and my youngest sister. Then, she passed away. In addition to the free counseling offered by USAA for social support and therapy, I started reading a lot and going back to church, learning to deal with it through the Lord.

Hardship and heartbreak have a way of leading us to God. I wasn't brought up in the church. Out of my family, I was the only one who wanted to go to church when I was little. My mom would dress me and send me every Sunday morning. It wasn't until my adult years, however, that I actually developed a personal relationship with God. I had my oldest daughter when I was seventeen, and when I was four-months pregnant, her father was incarcerated and sentenced to twenty-seven years to life, leaving me to raise her alone.

Then, I met my ex-husband Bernie. He was in the military. We married, but he turned out to be abusive. He would beat on me. Eventually, I left him. Yes, I am a domestic violence survivor as well. As the saying goes, if it wasn't one thing, it was another. Those same struggles that I went through in my life let me know that only God could get me out of them. I realized through studying, keeping a journal, and looking back through my notes that I had gone through the same stuff before. I started focusing more on the Lord and asking Him to give me strength to pull through. I developed a personal relationship with Him. I also began encouraging others who were doing far worse than I was—emotionally, physically, and financially—to develop a relationship with Him. When you realize that a whole lot of people are going through stuff worse than you, there's more room to talk about and share what you're going through with someone else.

A valuable lesson I learned was to release any should've, could've, and would'ves. Before my youngest sister died, she had been in so many rehabilitation centers in efforts to get her life together. Lish would always say she wanted to be home during the holidays, and every time we'd let her out, she would go home, get to drinking, and be right back there within the next month. It was tough. I prayed, and I prayed, and I prayed for God to make her better and to make a way for her. Through it all, she would tell me that she knew God and knew that He was taking care of her. "I'm okay. This is my life. Let me live it," she would say. I would cry and beg her to change, reminding her that it was just me and her left, but she was determined that it was her life. She had been through a lot, and she was already sick. She had been drinking so long, too, that she thought there was nothing left to do. I had to be at peace with that.

Another big epiphany I had was learning to be okay with not being okay. Sometimes you don't want to budge or go anywhere, and nothing is wrong with that. That's all a part of the grieving process, and you owe it to yourself to honor your feelings in that way. Knowing when to mother yourself, if you will, is also important. When it begins to feel as though the walls are closing in on you—when you're beyond sad, depressed, and drained, and feel as if you can't make it—you need to get out and be around other people. Otherwise, it's going to get worse. You also have to be willing to make the calls because others won't want to bother you during this time. They'll figure that you don't want to hang out. Learning to reach out, be it for emotional support, counseling, or a movie date, is important.

When I returned from Iraq, I was diagnosed with post-traumatic stress disorder (PTSD). The best parts of that experience were the relaxation therapy exercises and breathing techniques that I was taught. I learned how to stay calm in certain situations, how to manage my emotions, and how to control my thoughts. I'll be sharing some of these exercises and techniques with you in this section as we explore shock and denial, anger, bargaining, depression, and acceptance.

# Shock and Denial

Shock and denial are the first stage of grief. Shock is a natural reaction to loss. When you experience shock, your mind might become blank, and you may become confused. You will suffer from numbness. Other times, your symptoms could be severe. Your breathing might become labored. Your heart could race. You may even feel dizzy and light-headed. The best thing to do is to sit down. You must try to relax and calm your breathing. Shock is not trying to hurt you. It's trying to emotionally protect you from becoming overwhelmed with loss.

Denial is another natural mechanism for dealing with loss. It helps you avoid accepting your loss. Its function is to keep the pain and hurt away. Denial makes you believe many things, including that your loved one will come back to you. It can also have the opposite effect. It might make you not want to talk about the loss or even think about it.

Remember, shock and denial are mechanisms to handle a loss. They are not permanent—only temporary. They are the beginning of the grief and healing process. They are the foundation for hope and moving forward. An eagle symbolizes many things to many different people. To me, it symbolizes this hope. It isn't always easy to get past the denial because you have to deal with painful things. But I promise you, it's worth it.

The following devotionals are designed to bring you comfort, support, and a sense of understanding as you transition through this stage. Remember, however, that the five stages may not show up in this order in your life. You could very well experience anger prior to shock, and that's okay. Again, start with the section that best serves your needs at the time.

# DAY 1

## Thought

Denial is the first stage in the grief process. It's necessary to overcome denial so you can move through the other stages of the grief process: anger, bargaining, depression, and acceptance. Denial is healthy for a while. You're in denial when:

1. You wake up every morning and replay the tragic event in your mind, thinking it didn't really happen.

2. You can't stop thinking about the tragic event and can't properly function in your everyday life.

## Word

"Humble yourselves, therefore, under God's mighty hand, that he may lift you up in due time. Cast all your anxiety on him because he cares for you" (1 Peter 5:67 NIV).

## Prayer

God, I thank you for protecting me, even when I'm unaware of it, and for also having my best interest at heart. Though it's hard to believe that (insert name) is no longer with us, I trust that everything happens according to your divine plan.

## Challenge

Choose a positive feeling or memory involving your loved one that you hold dear. Maybe it was peace, laughter, closeness, warmth, forgiveness, etc. Lie down in a quiet area and visualize this feeling or memory as a light. If a particular color comes to mind, that's okay. Just be with it. Allow it to radiate through your being.

# DAY 2

## Thought

Denial is a mechanism to protect you from loss. It makes you question reality. Did the loss actually happen? Yes, it did, but it's not your fault. Your job is to embrace denial so that you can transition into the next stage of grief. There is no set timeframe for transitioning from denial. Take your time.

## Word

"And then this: We can tell you with complete confidence-- we have the Master's [W]ord—that when the Master comes again to get us, those of us who are still alive will not get a jump on the dead and leave them behind. In actual fact, they'll be ahead of us. The Master [H]imself will give the command. Archangel thunder! God's trumpet blast! He'll come down from heaven and the dead in Christ will rise— they'll go first. Then the rest of us who are still alive at the time will be caught up with them into the clouds to meet the Master. Oh, we'll be walking on air! And then there will be one huge family reunion with the Master. So reassure one another with these words" (1 Thessalonians 4:15-18).

## Prayer

Dear Lord, this loss hasn't been easy. I struggle to come to terms with it. Please help me accept what seems impossible and guide me with your Divine grace. Amen.

## Challenge

Sit quietly and accept the impossible. Embrace your fond memories. Vow that you will overcome denial—in your own time and on your own terms.

# DAY 3

## Thought

Denial is a coping mechanism. It helps you with ongoing trauma such as abuse and addiction. When you deny that these problems exist, you feel like you don't have to deal with them. You're in this type of denial when you make excuses for these problems, when you don't want to think about them, and when you ignore the facts.

## Word

"For freedom Christ has set us free; stand firm therefore, and do not submit again to a yoke of slavery" (Galatians 5:1 ESV).

## Prayer

God, I understand that anything that I cannot release has power over me. I no longer want to be enslaved by my circumstances and problems. Instead, I choose to be free, in Your name and in your will. Help me to stand firmly in your word so that I can best serve and represent Your name. In Jesus's name, Amen.

## Challenge

If you can, sit on your hands. If not, simply place them in your lap, imagining them to be the seat of your being. Consider the ongoing problems that you're dealing with. Verbally, declare yourself free from each one.

# DAY 4

## Thought

Denial becomes unhealthy when you use it every day as a way to deal with reality. Set your soul free by acknowledging denial so you can live in truth. Work past denial by talking with trusted members of your inner circle about what's happening. When you think, "This can't be happening," say, "Yes, this is happening."

## Word

"These things God has revealed to us through the Spirit. For the Spirit searches everything, even the depths of God" (1 Corinthians 2:10).

## Prayer

Holy Spirit, I need You. Guide me into truth and reveal unto me all that I need to know when I need to know it. In Jesus's name, Amen.

## Challenge

Place your hands over your heart, press gently, and declare that all is well. Repeat this until you believe it in your spirit.

# Day 5

## Thought

Grief is a process. The numbing experience of denial ends when you acknowledge your loss. This will cause you to release pent up emotions. An emotional release is when you finally express your grief openly. This is natural and normal. Embrace it.

## Word

"For everything there is a season, a time for every activity under heaven. A time to be born and a time to die. A time to plant and a time to harvest. A time to kill and a time to heal. A time to tear down and a time to build up. A time to cry and a time to laugh. A time to grieve and a time to dance" (Ecclesiastes 3:1–4 NLT).

## Prayer

Father, thank you for helping me understand that mourning is natural and necessary for the healing process. Please help me to encourage emotional release and love unconditionally. In Jesus's name, Amen.

## Challenge

Sit or lie comfortably and begin focusing on your breath. Starting at your toes, visualize the unconditional love of God radiating through every centimeter of your being. Continue until your body is completely relaxed and your spirit restored.

# Day 6

## Thought

Prayer is a necessary part of the healing process. It's a state of being engaged with God. The world is a hard place to live in. You must take the good with the bad, the laughter with the tears. God knows what you're going through and remembers you.

During my mom's experience with cancer, prayer was my lifeline to God. Every time I prayed, I was in His presence. This changed my life forever.

## Word

"Always be joyful. Never stop praying. Be thankful in all circumstances, for this is God's will for you who belong to Christ Jesus" (1 Thessalonians 5:16–18– NLV).

## Prayer

Father, there are times that I feel I have no control over my emotions and feel overtaken; my body sweats, and my hands shake at the thought of an unknown fear. Please keep me strong during these times and let me know that You are by my side, helping me face my fears and overcome. Amen.

## Challenge

Today, write your prayers instead of verbalizing. You may find that it takes your spiritual practice to another level. Don't pause to think or get your wording "right." Just write, coming to God exactly as you are.

# Day 7

## Thought

Sometimes people come into your life for a season, and they're not to continue you through the whole journey. You have to understand that the Lord has placed them there for a time such as this, and after you pass this time, through this season, they may part or pass.

## Word

"My flesh and my heart may fail, but God is the strength of my heart and my portion forever" (Psalm 73:26).

## Prayer

God, because You are with me, I have no reason to fear. Help me to stop worrying. Help me to relax and rest in the promises of Your word. I know You are with me because the Bible says so. I also know You will never give me more than I can handle. Lord, thank You for giving me the faith to trust You in this situation, and the strength of character I need to get through it in perfect obedience to Your word. I pray right now for Your wisdom and guidance, and Your favor and protection. And in the name of Jesus, I receive Your peace. In Jesus's name, Amen.

## Challenge

Sit or lie comfortably. Close your eyes and begin to scan your body for tension. Start with your toes and slowly work your way to the top of your head. Wherever there is stress in your body, take a moment to breathe into that space. Replace the tension with faith and gratitude. Continue until you feel completely at peace.

# DAY 8

## Thought

I often look for inspiration and consolation from the Whisper of God website. The following passage may be helpful to you:

> Feeling like you're being overwhelmed? Your ability to weather life's storms rests on your ability to go through them with God. You may be in rough water but He won't let you drown. You need to keep moving forward and trust that during this time He is working to bring about a brighter future for you. We may not know the day that future might arrive, but stay strong and have confidence that it is coming.

God hasn't forgotten about you. He's making a way for you. Don't let the overwhelming feeling of grief hold you back. Stay strong, and you will be rewarded.

## Word

"Yes, my soul, find rest in God; my hope comes from him. Truly he is my rock and my salvation; he is my fortress, I will not be shaken. My salvation and my honor depend on God; he is my mighty rock, my refuge. Trust in him at all times, you people; pour out your hearts to him, for God is our refuge" (Psalm 62:5–8 NIV).

## Prayer

Dear God, I know that You are working to bring a new day to me. A day that is brighter and more peaceful than the days I am seeing now. It's only through trusting in You that I am able to tread the rough waters without drowning, as I wait patiently for the dawn of that new day to come. Amen.

## Challenge

Common places where stress hides include our neck, shoulders, lower back, and stomach. Where do you carry it? Place your hands in that spot (alternating if you have to) and ask God to restore your peace. Have a genuine heart-to-heart moment with Him, using your authentic voice.

# DAY 9

## Thought

At some point, we all become overwhelmed with grief, anxiety, or stress. You don't and shouldn't have to deal with it alone. Some people you can turn to for help include licensed professionals, life coaches, spiritual advisors, or trusted friends and family members.

## Word

"Where there is no guidance, a people falls, but in an abundance of counselors there is safety" (Proverbs 11:14 ESV).

## Prayer

Dear God, thank You for Your grace and for never forsaking Your promises. Lead me in Your ways and help me to see and love those around me as You do. Guide my footsteps for Your glory. I want every decision, thought, and spoken word to match Your will. In Jesus's name, Amen.

## Challenge

It's best to identify help before you need it. Take a moment to research outreach programs, support groups, or therapists in your area with whom you would feel comfortable consulting, should the need arise. Keep this contact information in a safe place.

# DAY 10

## Thought

Grief, shock, denial, and fear can keep us from living a normal life and cause anxiety. More often than not, this anxiety is worse than the actual problem. God won't let you succumb to the worry. You can only be defeated by these emotions when you separate yourself from God.

## Word

"Then you will know the truth, and the truth will set you free" (John 8:32 NIV).

## Prayer

God, grant me the strength to overcome denial. Reveal the truth to me, so I can embrace it. Amen.

## Challenge

If you continue to live in denial, you'll pay a price. You'll remain disappointed and angry, which will cause you to lose even more.

Let go of denial by:

1.  Determining why the situation is difficult to deal with.

2.  Opening your mind to see all of the evidence.

3. Asking God to reveal to you what you need so you can accept the truth.

4. Accepting the fact that the truth will set you free, even though it may not feel like it right now.

# ANGER

If you have lost a loved one, you have a very long and hard journey ahead of you. Grief is exhausting, and anger is a messy stage in the healing process. Like denial, anger is normal and healthy. When you lose a loved one, it's heartbreaking. When someone you love dies, you may be angry with that person. You may become angry because the person that you were expecting to live the rest of your life with you has left. You may feel abandoned.

You may have been surprised at the death of your loved one. This kind of surprise often leads to anger. Every bereavement has its own set of sorrows and other strong emotions to go with it. There is the sorrow that comes suddenly and shockingly when someone dies unexpectedly. Then, there are the long sorrows with losing someone who has a terminal illness.

As you know, I have experienced them both after losing my loving companion Paul. I was devastated when he was killed in a car accident. He was not sick and was in good health. He was only forty-nine years old. I felt he still had plenty of time left. There were so many things that we didn't get to do. So many things left unfinished. Then, all of a sudden, he was gone. I felt forsaken, empty, lonely, and torn in two. I felt vulnerable and angry, too. I loved him and wasn't ready to let go so suddenly.

Anger is often expressed through those who were involved with the death in some manner. Some become angry with God or their higher power, as if God betrayed them. It's natural to feel this way, but please remember, God loves you. He is not punishing you. He is preparing you. Grief is temporary. Joy is forever. On the day of your death, you will enter paradise and be reunited with your loved ones. All you will know from then on is joy. When you are feeling angry because of loss, take the time to let it out, so you can move to the stage of grief. Be mindful that this too is only temporary.

# Day 11

## Thought

Are you able to forgive the person who hurt you? If you are, is it true forgiveness or are you just going through the motions? You must be able to truly forgive that person. It has to come from your heart so you aren't emotionally tied to that experience anymore. God has shown you how to forgive—learn from Him so that you can be set free.

## Word

"You have heard that it was said, 'Love your neighbor and hate your enemy.' But I tell you, love your enemies and pray for those who persecute you, that you may be children of your Father in heaven" (Matthew 5:43–45).

## Prayer

Father, letting go of the hurt is the hardest part. I can keep someone out of my life so they don't hurt me again, but I can't block out the emotions that live within me every day. The hurt turns to sadness or anger, and the sadness and anger keep me from moving forward. Please let me learn to forgive the way You do, so I can look forward with hopeful anticipation towards the wonderful future You have in store for me. Amen.

## Challenge

Go before a mirror, place a hand over your heart, and release. In your reflection, you're not only seeing yourself, but you're also seeing your loved ones, those who hurt you, and God Himself. Here's a jump-start: "Forgiving myself, or another, allows my brain to stop releasing stressful chemicals in my body." I can now let go of the past, and with it, anger, guilt, and sadness. I can live more fully in the fullness and expression of life.

# DAY 12

## Thought

There are always choices and options. I can obey the Lord, love Him with all my heart, soul, and mind, and reap rewards and victory, or I can ignore Him and suffer the consequences of defeat.

## Word

"Finally, brothers, whatever is true, whatever is honorable, whatever is just, whatever is pure, whatever is lovely, whatever is commendable, if there is any excellence, if there is anything worthy of praise, think about these things" (Philippians 4:8 ESV).

## Prayer

Lord God, You are powerful and loving, and I adore You. Help me to choose Your blessings, choose Your victory, and walk with You every moment of my life. In Jesus's name, Amen.

## Challenge

Are your choices leading to victory or defeat? Examine your relationship with the Lord. Are you seeking wholehearted devotion of Him?

# DAY 13

## Thought

It is your choice to forgive. You might not be able to forgive the hurt, but you can move on and let go of the bitterness, the anger, and the need for justice or revenge. How do you accomplish this? By trusting in God and letting Him take over your need for judgment. Surrender your negative feelings.

## Word

"Do not judge, and you will not be judged. Do not condemn, and you will not be condemned. Forgive, and you will be forgiven" (Luke 6:37 NIV.)

## Prayer

Father, please help me triumph over the hurt and let go of long-term anger. I turn this situation over to You and trust that You'll handle it, so I can move forward with my life in a happy and healthy way. Amen.

## Challenge

Being angry or hurt by someone else teaches you something about yourself. How have you been offended or hurt? In turn, what does that mean you stand for? What value of yours was crossed? Explore this in your journal in order to fully grasp your thoughts and beliefs.

# DAY 14

## Thought

It's extremely important to exercise regularly, especially when you're angry, as it gives a place for all of that energy to go. In addition to sustaining your health, exercise also helps to relieve tension and stress. You can work out at home, in the gym, outside, etc. Be sure not to overdo it and cause injury, and if you have any doctor's restrictions, please adhere to them.

## Word

"Or do you not know that your body is a temple of the Holy Spirit within you, whom you have from God? You are not your own, for you were bought with a price. So glorify God in your body" (1 Corinthians 6:19–20 ESV).

## Prayer

Lord God, give me the strength and wisdom to honor the body that You blessed me with. It's my temple and deserves to be treated as such, so that I can live out Your calling over my life. Thank You for caring for me and loving me the way You do. In Jesus's name, Amen.

## Challenge

Using your phone or an actual calendar, block out time to exercise for the next seven days. For additional accountability, tell a friend or set an alarm to remind you.

# Day 15

## Thought

With God, every day is a chance for a new beginning. No matter who we are or what we have going on in our lives, God holds out His hand and waits for us to take it. With Him, the opportunities for healing are endless. Take God's hand, release anger, and begin to heal.

## Word

"When my heart was grieved and my spirit embittered, I was senseless and ignorant; I was a brute beast before you. Yet I am always with you; you hold me by my right hand. You guide me with your counsel, and afterward you will take me into glory. Whom have I in heaven but you? And earth has nothing I desire besides you" (Psalm 73:21–25 NIV).

## Prayer

Lord, there are times when the hurt placed on me by others becomes too much, and I want to see the other person pay for the hurt they've caused me. I get stuck thinking about this, and I find myself unable to move forward in a healthy and full way. Father, I turn my hurt over to You so I can start to move forward towards a new day, and You can deal with those that have hurt me as You, only in Your judgment, see fit. Amen.

## Challenge

Meditate on the following affirmation: "I am at peace with the will of God."

# Day 16

## Thought

God never promised you an easy life, but He did promise you that He would never leave you. When bitterness tries to take over your life, trust in God to help you through it. Don't succumb to the bitterness and resist the prompting of the Holy Spirit. Recognize your shortcomings, repent, and humble yourself, so God can heal your bitterness.

## Word

"I will give you a new heart and put a new spirit in you; I will remove from you your heart of stone and give you a heart of flesh" (Ezekiel 36:26).

## Prayer

Jesus! Please give me the wisdom to overcome hurt. Show me the path to forgiveness, how to be humble, and how to be still, so that I may absorb Your gifts. In the name of Jesus, Amen.

## Challenge

Close your eyes and place your hands over your heart. Meditate on the following affirmation: "I forgive those who've hurt me."

# Day 17

## Thought

Bitterness can affect anyone at any time. It may start as a small seed planted in your spirit, but it can grow into a tree if left unresolved. Don't let anger, a bad attitude, jealousy, or disappointment take control of your spirit. Here is another excerpt from the Whisper of God website:

> There are times when God has something great waiting for you just beyond your reach that you will need to go outside of your comfort zone to realize. Don't let any self-doubt hold you back from realizing what He has in store for you.

## Word

"Create in me a pure heart, O God, and renew a steadfast spirit within me" (Psalm 51:10).

## Prayer

Dear God, please help me to forgive (insert name). Please help me relinquish the anger and bitterness I'm feeling, so that I may walk in your grace. Please guide me through this experience and help me heal. Thank You, and in Jesus's mighty name, I pray. Amen.

## Challenge

This meditation will take place in the shower. When you first step in, take a few deep breaths. Forgive yourself for any feelings of bitterness, anger, and resentment. Claim peace and joy over your life, and imagine all negative emotions washing away.

# Day 18

## Thought

May God destroy all of your lies. The sin that is anger may have a strong grip on your heart. Trying to overcome anger in the past and failing causes a feeling of hopelessness. Acknowledging this sin and revealing the truth about anger will give you the strength and confidence to overcome any problem.

## Word

"He who is slow to anger has great understanding, But he who is quick-tempered exalts folly" (Proverbs 14:29 NASB).

## Prayer

Father, help me feel Your grace. Guide me through the valley of the shadow of death and fill me with the Holy Spirit. I need You now more than ever. In Jesus's name, Amen.

## Challenge

Send tension out of your body through your fingertips. Stretch your arms out to the sides away from your body and release the tension.

# Day 19

## Thought

Live righteously by acknowledging the connection between God's ways and peace. To be in perfect peace, you must let go of anger and depression.

## Word

"Jesus said, 'Let the little children come to me and do not hinder them, for to such belongs the kingdom of heaven.'" (Matthew 19:14 ESV).

## Prayer

Lord, please take all the anger away from me. Allow me to fill my spirit with all of the good and positive things in my life. Explore my heart and eradicate anything that may hurt me, so that I may be free. Amen.

## Challenge

Do a few minutes of even meditative breathing to calm the body-mind. *Example:* breathe in, one one thousand; breathe out, one one thousand; breathe in, one one thousand count and continue.

# Day 20

## Thought

Accept that the past cannot be changed. Trust that God will heal you. Things happen to you that may cause pain and sadness to live within your heart. Don't let anger linger and make your heart hard.

## Word

"I will heal my people and will let them enjoy abundant peace and security" (Jeremiah 33:6 NIV).

## Prayer

Heavenly Father, I humbly turn to You to be healed. Remove the past hurts and sadness from my heart. Don't allow my heart to hold on to anger and prevent happiness. Amen.

## Challenge

Take a brisk walk for a few minutes or more. Swing your arms back and forth so that when your right foot steps forward, your left arm swings forward, and when your left footsteps forward, your right arm swings forward. Keep your breathing even, such as two steps, breathe in, two steps, breathe out. While walking, think about the reasons you get angry in the first place. Is it frustration with others or yourself?

# BARGAINING

Bargaining is about control. It's your attempt to negotiate with God. You make promises in the hopes of stopping the pain associated with loss. You want things to go back to normal, even though you know it can never happen.

Bargaining is a natural part of the grief and healing process. Before it gets better, it will get worse. You might go as far as to question what you could've done differently. Do not fight these thoughts—they will help you accept the loss and transition into the next stage of grief.

I experienced the stage of bargaining with my sister, Lish. I loved her with all my heart. She was bipolar and would have bouts of depression. Suffering with these issues caused her to have moments of rage and despair. Other times, she was the sweetest person in the world. I used to ask the Lord to heal her. I knew I was trying to bargain with the Lord. I'd say, "Lord if you heal my sister, I will do anything for you." I was willing to give my right arm or right leg to heal Alicia. I suffered immensely with her. When she hurt, I hurt. I did not want to lose her. She was my baby sister. I used to call her "Baby Girl."

The stages of grief are not linear. You may start out in the first stage of grief, and then transition into stage four, only to return to stage one. They also don't have a specific duration. The stages of grief are a response to feelings. Each person responds to these feelings for different amounts of time.

Guilt is often bargaining's companion. You think, "if only I could've done something differently." You find fault with yourself, so that you don't have to feel the pain. You bargain with the pain, trying to negotiate your way out of the hurt.

# DAY 21

## Thought

Many believe grief comes from dealing with someone's death, but grief can come from many things (such as a break-up, the loss of a friend, or even the running away of a pet). The same bargaining phase may happen for someone dealing with any of these types of grief.

## Word

"Don't bargain with God. Be direct. Ask for what you need. This isn't a cat-and-mouse, hide-and-seek game we're in" (Matthew 7:7–8 MSG).

## Prayer

Dear Lord, I want very much to ask You to bring back what was, but instead I ask that You help me come to terms with what is. Help me heal and learn to love the life that has been given, even if it's not what I want. In Christ's name, Amen.

## Challenge

For all meditations, it's important to be relaxed and as calm as possible. Slow your breathing. For this meditation, imagine yourself buried up to your neck in sand. Your body can't move. This represents the burden of the grief you carry. Now imagine the sand rolling off your body; your body is getting lighter. This will help to clear and lighten your mind.

# Day 22

## Thought

It's easy to abandon friends and loved ones during this time. Seek out the comfort offered to you by those closest to you.

## Word

"Again you have heard that it was said to those of old, 'You shall not swear falsely, but shall perform to the Lord what you have sworn.' But I say to you, do not take an oath at all, either by heaven, for it is the throne of God, or by the earth, for it is his footstool, or by Jerusalem, for it is the city of the great King. And do not take an oath by your head, for you cannot make one hair white or black. Let what you say be simply 'Yes' or 'No'; anything more than this comes from evil" (Matthew 5:33–37 ESV).

## Prayer

Dear Lord, thank You for the day You have given me. Forgive me for holding onto what was and allow me to feel the peace that passes all understanding. Thank You, Father, Amen.

## Challenge

Dealing with grief is tiring, but during this stage, it's important to face what has happened in order to move on. Dwell on the events that brought you here, and release the pain through meditation, rather than bargaining with a higher power or other to deal with this stage.

# DAY 23

## Thought

It's important to remember that it's perfectly normal to want things to go back to the way they were before the loss took place. It's important to remember you will grieve as deeply as you loved. The old saying, "Time heals all wounds," is something to remember. It takes time to heal. Allow yourself time to go through the process. That is why it is important to have good memories with your loved ones. Remember that time is worth more than money.

## Word

"God is not man, that he should lie, or a son of man, that he should change his mind. Has he said, and will he not do it? Or has he spoken, and will he not fulfill it?" (Numbers 23:19)

## Prayer

Dear Lord, thank You for everything You give me each day. Thank You for the air in my lungs. Even though I wish for much more, I know that You will take care of me through this trying time. Thank You for all You provide, Amen.

## Challenge

Imagine yourself as a great stone statue, stiff and warmed by the sun. As the sun warms you, you begin to become loose and free. Now, you're more like clay. You're malleable.

Continue to let the stiffness of your body wash away until you are like jelly, and your body and mind are more comfortable and more relaxed.

# DAY 24

**Thought**

It's okay to feel a very wide range of emotions. You may be sad, angry, hurt, or even relieved. You may even experience a mix of these emotions. You'll often change back and forth between them. This is normal, and you deserve this time to feel these emotions.

**Word**

"Blessed are those who mourn, for they will be comforted" (Matthew 5:4 NIV).

**Prayer**

Dear Lord, please forgive my weakness and show me strength. Give me the strength to move forward. Thank You for all the love and compassion You show me everyday. Amen.

**Challenge**

Imagine you're carrying four buckets of water: one on each shoulder, one in each hand. Now, imagine slowly pouring the water out of the bucket from your left shoulder. Feel the weight lift off of you. Now, your right shoulder. Feel the cool water splash against you as the weight leaves your stressed shoulders. Now, free each hand by pouring out the water. You're now lighter and freed.

# Day 25

## Thought

Wanting to bargain is normal, but it's important to realize that bargaining won't bring back what was lost, and in some cases, that's for the better. Even if it doesn't seem like it now.

## Word

"Praise be to the God and Father of our Lord Jesus Christ, the Father of compassion and the God of all comfort, who comforts us in all our troubles, so that we can comfort those in any trouble with the comfort we ourselves receive from God" (2 Corinthians 1:3–4).

## Prayer

Heavenly Father, thank You for another day. I fight the temptation to promise things beyond my being, so please continue to watch over me and comfort me. Wrap me in Your loving arms and protect me. Thank You for all You give me, Amen.

## Challenge

Close your eyes and focus on the following affirmation: "I accept the flow of life. It brings me joy."

# DAY 26

## Thought

Avoid false hope that might be given by others in an effort to help. This will only set you back in the grieving process, not move you forward.

## Word

"So do not fear, for I am with you; do not be dismayed, for I am your God. I will strengthen you and help you; I will uphold you with my righteous right hand" (Isaiah 41:10).

## Prayer

Dear Lord, I come to You because I am hurting, scared, and I wish to turn to You and be embraced at this time by Your loving arms. Please surround me in light and love. Amen.

## Challenge

Have you ever seen a lava lamp? Have you touched the base when it was cold, or swirled the jelly-like lump at the bottom around? Imagine you're the colored oils in a lava lamp. What color are you? Imagine the lava lamp has not been turned on yet. You're cold, hard, and complacent. Now, imagine someone turns the lamp on underneath you. You begin to warm up. Now, you feel softer, lighter. Imagine you continue to become lighter until you're flowing, breaking apart, lighter, and free.

# Day 27

## Thought

Bargaining feels right, but it give you false hope, and shouldn't be reciprocated.

## Word

"God is our refuge and strength, an ever-present help in trouble. Therefore we will not fear, though the earth give way and the mountains fall into the heart of the sea" (Psalm 46:1–2).

## Prayer

Dear God, please continue to watch over me, protect me, guide me, and hold me as I fight the urge to bargain for what I want instead of taking what You have given me. Forgive me for fighting the plan You have for me. Amen.

## Challenge

Imagine you are a dandelion, white and fuzzy. Imagine blowing in the breeze. Now, your fuzzy seedlings begin to drift away in the wind. Imagine they are your worries, your troubles, and your cares being blown away by the wind.

# Day 28

## Thought

Bargaining can be one of the most difficult stages to go through in the grieving process. This is mostly due to the fact that hope usually is not returned the way we wish it was.

## Word

"My comfort in my suffering is this: Your promise preserves my life" (Psalm 119:50).

## Prayer

Dear Lord, I am struggling and I need Your help. I ask that You hold me in Your hands. I give all of my troubles to You and will follow Your guidance. Bless me, and protect me. Amen.

## Challenge

While concentrating on things that relieve you, that calm and soothe you, play relaxing music. Try to play something peaceful and tranquil.

# DAY 29

## Thought

You won't be able to simply "get over" whatever it is that you have lost. It will take time, but you'll learn to live with the loss you have suffered.

## Word

"The Lord is my rock, my fortress and my deliverer; my God is my rock, in whom I take refuge, my shield and the horn of my salvation, my stronghold"(Psalm 18:2).

## Prayer

Dear God, I ask that You bless me and my loved ones. Keep me safe and in Your loving arms. Protect me as I begin to fully grasp what has happened, what will happen, and what it will mean for my life. Thank You for Your love, Amen.

## Challenge

Instead of bargaining, try to focus on what happened and how it'll affect your life in the long run. Focus on the repercussions of your loss.

# DAY 30

## Thought

Sometimes the best thing you can do for yourself, at this stage, is point even more at the inevitable. Even though this may very well turn into depression (which may be a necessary move).

## Word

"Humble yourselves, therefore, under God's mighty hand, that he may lift you up in due time. Cast all your anxiety on him because he cares for you" (1 Peter 5:6–7).

## Prayer

Dear God, I am having a difficult time accepting what is. I wish for a different outcome and that circumstances were different. Please continue to be with me as I work through everything that I am feeling, and continue to lead me back to You. In the name of Jesus, Amen.

## Challenge

Call yourself to focus on what is and what will be. Meditate on how the events of the losses you have suffered have changed your life, and try to search the future.

# Depression

Everyone experiences a defining, life-altering event, where everything changes. For me, that defining event happened during a moment of pure grief. In a split second, I knew my life was about to change forever. In March of 1998, after a short bout with lung cancer, my mother, who was my best friend and confidante, passed. It was the worst day of my life.

Yet, even in a haze of grief, I knew something happened to me that day. I stood with my back against that hospital wall, praying for her to find peace. She had left me, but she had brought everyone so much joy and laughter. We had great memories. It was selfish for me to try and hold on to her, for she had become gravely ill and was really suffering.

I knew that I was now different from the person who walked into the hospital that day. Being a mother and grandmother just heightened and deepened everything I felt passionately about. Losing my mother took it to another level. I took it really hard after Mama died in those early days.

Depression is a normal stage to go through after having lost someone or something important to you. There are several symptoms of depression: sadness, regret, and guilt are just some of what you will experience. Depression will stop you.

You will feel as though the world has moved on and left you behind. Know that this is natural and healthy. Allow yourself time to move through depression.

There were a few particular challenges that helped me in this stage of grief. One, I challenged myself to feel. There were many days that I just felt numb. I knew, however, that if I needed to move on, it would require me to feel something—even if that meant crying one more time. I also challenged myself to hug someone. We oftentimes associate depression with being at our lowest point and don't want people to see us during that time. While it's okay—healthy, even—to spend time alone, it's also important to be around others. I spent a great deal of time with Lish, my family and other loved ones, counselors, and doctors. Finally, I focused on how I felt about the loss. Even when I couldn't be honest about it with others, I made sure that I was honest with myself. This helped me tremendously in moving forward.

While this section supports you in picking up the pieces, it also serves as your source of understanding. Use it as a shoulder to lean on and permission to embrace your feelings however they show up. It's okay.

# Day 31

## Thought

Society views depression as unnatural and something that needs to be "fixed" immediately. Contrary to this popular belief, depression is a natural part of the healing process. When you find yourself deep in depression filled with stress and anxiety, it's time to take a break. Instead of thinking of the horrors of death, think of the freeing power that our mortal life gives us once we enter the gates of heaven. Spend time with God away from the day-to-day demands that are draining you. Let Him reenergize you, so that you may return to your life filled with peace.

## Word

"He refreshes my soul. Even though I walk through the shadow of death, I will fear no evil, for you are with me; your rod and your staff, they comfort me" (Psalm 23:3–4 ESV).

## Prayer

You, Lord, are what keeps me going when the days get tough. It's the time that I get to spend alone with You that keeps my mind clear and my soul refreshed. Amen.

## Challenge

Imagine yourself covered in mud. On your chest is a large, dried ball of clay. No matter how you try to move it, you cannot breathe and you cannot move it. Then, it begins to rain. The rain hits you in the face like a cool ocean breeze. The rain begins to wash away the mud and clay ball. Slowly, you can feel yourself breathe more comfortably until it's all washed away and you feel lighter.

# DAY 32

## Thought

Loss is deeply depressing. Depression, like the other stages of grief, is natural and healthy. Not experiencing depression after loss is unusual.

## Word

"Then we which are alive and remain shall be caught up together with them in the clouds, to meet the Lord in the air: and so shall we ever be with the Lord. Wherefore comfort one another with these words" (1 Thessalonians 4:17).

## Prayer

Dear God, I am feeling hurt, alone, scared, and weak. Please take over my life and consume my grief. Help me through this troubling time. Amen.

## Challenge

Imagine you have an orange lodged in your throat. The orange will not come out, and you can feel it blocking your air. Then, the orange starts to shrink. Slowly, the orange becomes smaller and you can breathe better. Eventually, the orange becomes so small, you no longer feel it in your throat. You can breathe easily. Breathe. Keep breathing.

# DAY 33

## Thought

Depression is a unique stage in the grieving process. You might feel isolated and alone. Move through this stage at your own pace. Know that you are not alone. God is by your side.

## Word

"For he has not despised or scorned the suffering of the afflicted one; he has not hidden his face from him but has listened to his cry for help" (Psalm 22:24).

## Prayer

Dear God, there are times when I feel so sad and alone. During these times I wonder if anyone can know how I feel. When I feel like this, I remember the sadness You faced and the tears You shed, and I realize You know how I feel. I also know that I am never alone, for You are always with me. Amen

## Challenge

Imagine plunging to the bottom of the sea. You can see the light shining through the water breaking at the top, but you can't seem to get any closer. Slowly, you begin to float. You can feel your legs begin to move and your arms aren't quite so heavy. You get closer and closer to the light, and then, finally break the surface. You take in large gulps of air, and then, smaller ones, until you're calm and still, floating on the surface.

# DAY 34

## Thought

Depression has only recently been seen as a normal function of the grieving cycle, so don't let others tell you how long you should be depressed.

## Word

"One thing I ask from the Lord, this only do I seek: that I may dwell in the house of the Lord all the days of my life, to gaze on the beauty of the Lord and to seek him in his temple. For in the day of trouble he will keep me safe in his dwelling; he will hide me in the shelter of his sacred tent and set me high upon a rock" (Psalm 27:4–5).

## Prayer

Dear God, I ask that You bless me and my loved ones. Keep me safe and in Your loving arms. Protect me as I begin to fully grasp what has happened, what will happen, and what it will mean for my life. If I sink lower into my horrible feelings, please continue to pull me back out. Thank You for Your love, Amen.

## Challenge

Picture yourself in a room. It has no windows, no doors, no way in or out. Imagine it's soundproof. You can't hear the whistling of birds, the clatter of cars, or dogs barking in the distance. Breathe in . . . breathe out. Repeat.

# DAY 35

## Thought

This depressive state will feel as if it will never end, but it's important to understand that this is a normal stage and not a sign of any mental illness.

## Word

"For his anger lasts only a moment, but his favor lasts a lifetime; weeping may stay for the night, but rejoicing comes in the morning" (Psalm 30:5).

## Prayer

Dear God, I am having a difficult time accepting what is. I wish for a different outcome and that circumstances were different. The constant thought of what I have lost is pressing on my mind. Please ease my pain as I allow You to work in my life. In the name of Jesus, Amen.

## Challenge

Consider using yoga as one of your meditation techniques. Yoga is very soothing and healthy, both of which can be extremely helpful in this time of grieving.

# DAY 36

## Thought

It's okay to be sad. It's okay to feel overwhelmed. It's okay to cry.

## Word

"The righteous cry out, and the Lord hears them; he delivers them from all their troubles" (Psalm 34:17).

## Prayer

Dear God, please help me heal and learn to love the life that has been given, even if it's not what I want. Even when I begin to sink into a pit of anger and frustration, please hold tight to my heart. In Christ's name, Amen.

## Challenge

Allow yourself to let it all out. Focus on the good, the bad, and everything about the person or thing you lost. Allow it to all flow out of you.

# DAY 37

## Thought

You're not alone. It'll feel like you're alone, but you're not. Reach out to your friends, family, and community resources.

## Word

"But you, Lord, are a shield around me, my glory, the One who lifts my head high" (Psalm 3:3 NIV).

## Prayer

Dear God, I'm feeling isolated and alone. I feel left behind. Please help me during this time. I know I'm not truly alone because you are with me. Guide me through depression with your infinite wisdom. Amen.

## Challenge

Sit in your room with the curtains drawn and a Do Not Disturb sign on your door. Light a candle and relax. Listen to the sound of your own heartbeat. Try to breathe in rhythm with your heart.

# DAY 38

## Thought

It's in this stage that you begin to feel the true extent of what was lost, so know that it's okay to be emotional and tired. During these times I eat better. I make smoothies from fruits and vegetables, which help you to not be drained during this process. I also turn off all the lights when sleeping and turn off the television or cell phones near my bed. I try and sleep in total darkness. It helps me rest much better.

## Word

"So do not fear, for I am with you; do not be dismayed, for I am your God. I will strengthen you and help you; I will uphold you with my righteous right hand" (Isaiah 41:10).

## Prayer

Dear God, I know that You will take care of me through this trying time, even when I don't feel that I will ever get out of the horrible rut that I am in. Some days, life is just hard. In your word it says You will never leave me nor forsake me. I Am trusting You Lord. Thank You for all You provide, Amen.

## Challenge

If you find being in complete silence unnerving, you can play some soft, soothing music. This can filter out background noise if you live in a busy house and are unable to find a completely quiet spot. You can also purchase healing and meditating CDs in which I sell on my website: www. Griefhelpline.coach.

# DAY 39

## Thought

Common signs of depression are trouble sleeping, poor or no appetite, tiredness or lack of energy, and crying spells. These are all normal for someone grieving.

## Word

¹ I love You, O Lᴏʀᴅ, my strength.

² The Lᴏʀᴅ is my rock and my fortress and my deliverer;

My God, my strength, in whom I will trust;

My shield and the horn of my salvation, my stronghold.

³ I will call upon the Lᴏʀᴅ, *who is worthy* to be praised;

So shall I be saved from my enemies.

⁴ The pangs of death surrounded me,

And the floods of ungodliness made me afraid.

⁵ The sorrows of Sheol surrounded me;

The snares of death confronted me.

⁶ In my distress I called upon the Lᴏʀᴅ,

And cried out to my God;

He heard my voice from His temple,

And my cry came before Him, *even* to His ears.

(Psalms 18 1–6 ESV)

## Prayer

Dear Lord, please forgive my weakness and show me strength. Give me the strength to move forward and not fall into a permanent rut by keeping my mind fixed on you Lord. I will trust thee in the process Lord. Keep my heart calm and at peace. Lord grant me the peace that surpasses all understanding. In Your name, Amen.

## Challenge

Walk outside to meditate. Listen to the world around you. Breathe in through your nose and out through your mouth. Try to pick out different sounds around you as you do this. Everyone grieves differently. Don't be afraid to be vulnerable during this time. Open yourself up to the healing process. Cry if you must. Sing if you want to. Dance as if no one is watching. Above all else, do what feels natural to you. Claim your joy.

# DAY 40

## Thought

Grieving is necessary. Allow yourself to feel the pain of loss. Be willing to mourn with all of your soul, so that you may accept the painful truth. You may feel lonely or isolated. Many times during this stage people feel empty, numb, lost, or anxious. Remember that these things will pass. Don't let these feelings consume you.

## Word

"For I know the plans I have for you, declares the LORD, plans for welfare and not for evil, to give you a future and a hope" (Jeremiah 29:11 ESV).

## Prayer

Dear Lord, keep my heart calm and protected. Give me strength in the midst of this storm and allow my soul to be relieved of the grief that is consuming my body. Lord, You said I should put all my cares on You. Today I bring You my stress and burdens, and I leave them at Your feet. I am trusting You for strength, guidance, and wisdom. You are the way. Lord, You lead and I will follow. Today I find peace and relief from grief. In the name of Jesus, Amen.

## Challenge

To meditate on grief, let yourself sit alone by the water. To me water is relaxing, so I hope it helps you to just lay in the sun and listen to the waves. Looking at the sunrise or sunset on a beach is nature at its finest. Focus on your memories. Let them unfold naturally and let the feelings associated with your loss consume you. Pain, tears, anger, love, fear, and sorrow—let them wash over you like waves. As they reseed, breathe out and release them.

# ACCEPTANCE

Most people feel that acceptance of one's grief means being okay with what has happened. The truth is, some people may never be okay or all right with what has occurred in their lives. Acceptance means that one has finally come to the point in their grief that they accept the reality of what has occurred to be true. Let your grief go. You do not need to hold on to it anymore. Honor it and then release it.

Once you feel yourself come to terms with what has happened, rather than avoiding it or disbelieving, then you'll know you've started to broach this stage. It'll still be hard, and you'll have to learn to readjust your life, but you'll no longer attempt to push the truth away.

This isn't a "once you're there, it's all over," type of situation. The other stages will pop up from time to time. You may want to revert back to denial to ease the pain. Realizing and accepting the situation may throw you back into depression. You'll continue to feel the pain of these other stages.

I think Paul's death was the hardest for me to accept because he was killed in a car accident—he wasn't sick; it was a shock. Most of my family members' deaths were due to illnesses, so I was able to be there for them. I had more time to process what was happening and come to some level of acceptance before they were gone. I was able to be there for them because I had a warning, in a way. With Paul's sudden death, I felt helpless. Paul was my life partner. He was my friend, lover, and confidante for over thirty years. We were never married, but to me, we were soulmates. He was always there for me, and then one day, POOF! He was gone. He was a wonderful guy, and everybody loved him. Paul had a sense of humor and good looks—he was tall, dark, and handsome. I just loved my Pauly—that is what I used to call him. He truly was a great guy.

It's perfectly natural to feel like you may never accept the truth, especially at the beginning of your grieving. It takes some people longer to accept the reality than it does others. Trying to bottle it all up won't help. This doesn't allow your mind and body to grieve properly. You'll end up doing more damage to your body and psyche than if you were to allow yourself to feel. God guided me through my grieving and healing process. Through Him, I was able to release pent-up emotions. I was able to move forward on my path to joy.

# DAY 41

## Thought

Acceptance is the final stage, but remember that the other stages will crop back up during this stage, so don't expect to finally accept the situation and think that will be the end of it. You may feel self-pity. You may feel lonely or isolated. Many times during this stage people still feel empty, numb, lost, or anxious. Remember that these things will pass. Don't let these feelings consume you.

## Word

"For as in Adam we all die, also in Christ all will be made alive" (1 Corinthians 15:22).

## Prayer

Lord, my emotions have taken over me. I'm filled with sadness and depression. They're weighing me down. Please rescue me and remain with me during this difficult time. Amen.

## Challenge

Imagine you're floating in a pool. At first you fight the rocking of the waves, but as you drift farther out, the waves become less harsh. You can feel yourself giving in to the pull of the waves.

# Day 42

## Thought

Acceptance doesn't mean you are okay with the situation.

## Word

"If you do well, will not your countenance be lifted up? And if you do not do well, sin is crouching at the door; and its desire is for you, but you must rule over it" (Genesis 4:7).

## Prayer

Lord, I long for what I have lost, I miss my loved ones, and my heart aches. My loss is overwhelming, and I seemed to be consumed by the grief. My mind is racing, and I am experiencing emotional numbness. My grief tries to influence most of my waking moments. Help me to relax, feel less pain, and accept what is. Amen.

## Challenge

One way to meditate is to combine music with yoga. Relaxing music and stretching is a great way to focus and think about what has happened and become relaxed while thinking about the situation. Try Soaking music to experience healing, forgiveness, and renewed joy.

# DAY 43

## Thought

Acceptance means you accept the reality of what has happened, even though it's painful.

God gave his only begotten son so that we could live and live life more abundantly, Jesus sacrifi ed his life so we could have a better life. Find joy in knowing because of Him we live.

## Word

"Opening his mouth, Peter said: 'I most certainly understand now that God is not one to show partiality, but in every nation the man who fears Him and does what is right is welcome to Him" (Acts 10:34–35).

## Prayer

Precious Lord, help me process my loss. The wounds won't go away. Lord, allow the grief to have less power to dictate my life as I heal. Help me move forward. Help me to accept what has happened and not fall away from You because of it. Amen.

## Challenge

Focus on the reality of what has happened. It's painful to think about, but breathe in through your nose and out through your mouth. Concentrate on letting go of the pain as you face the situation. Come into His presence and lift up the name of Jesus.

# Day 44

## Thought

People will sometimes expect you to reach the stage of acceptance quickly, but reach it in your own time.

## Word

"Let the words of my mouth and the meditation of my heart Be acceptable in Your sight, O LORD, my rock and my Redeemer" (Psalm 19:14).

## Prayer

Lord, help me to welcome JOY into my life to replace the pain. Help me to experience a JOY filled life again, without the overwhelming sorrow from what has occurred. Amen.

## Challenge

Instead of the "why," focus on what happened. Many times we cannot come up with why something happened, but we can focus on what happened and accept that reality.

# DAY 45

## Thought

Remember that accepting the reality of the situation doesn't mean you're abandoning your love for the person or thing lost. It won't make the hurt go away.

## Word

"First of all, then, I urge that entreaties and prayers, petitions and thanksgivings, be made on behalf of all men" (1 Timothy 2:1).

## Prayer

Lord, help me to draw nearer to You, rather than further away. It's easy to want to be angry and blame others at this time. Please give me the peace that surpasses all understanding. Amen.

## Challenge

Breathing deeply slows the heart rate, relaxes the muscles, and focuses the mind. It is an ideal way to begin practice. Focus your breathing and relax as you think about past events.

# DAY 46

## Thought

Acceptance is a necessary yet painful step. In order to achieve acceptance, you must constantly face the reality of the situation, which can be excruciating.

## Word

"To the praise of the glory of His grace, which He freely bestowed on us in the Beloved" (Ephesians 1:6).

## Prayer

Lord, You are my hope and my salvation through this dark time. Don't leave or forsake me during this time of trouble and need. I ask this in Your name, Amen.

## Challenge

Meditate on the present. What other things are going on in your life? What other events can you and should you focus on right now in order to return to even a small bit of normalcy?

# DAY 47

## Thought

Don't be disappointed or upset when you don't immediately get to acceptance. It's important to go through all the other stages in order to reach acceptance in a healthy manner.

## Word

"For we do not have a high priest who is unable to sympathize with our weaknesses, but one who in every respect has been tempted as we are, yet without sin" (Hebrews 4:15 ESV).

## Prayer

Lord, by day I pour out my heartbreak to You. At night, I give You my racing thoughts that keep me awake and prevent me from finding peace. I give it all to You and ask You to guide my life. Strengthen me Lord—I know You will never leave me or forsake me. I need You now, Jesus. Amen.

## Challenge

The art of focusing your attention on a single point is hard work, and you have to really put your mind to it. Think of the future. Right now, it might be hard to see where you'll be in a few days, weeks, months, or even years, but try to picture what good will be found in your life.

# Day 48

## Thought

Accepting the reality of the situation can be difficult and painful. Hang in there.

## Word

"Jesus wept" (John 11:35).

## Prayer

Lord, I take refuge in You and I will not be afraid. I know You will guide me through this darkness. Love me, hold me, care for me. Amen.

## Challenge

Focus on being alive. Take notice of each of your body parts. Pay attention to your toes, then feet, and move up from there. Take notice of your internal organs, moving and working. This is a healthy way to remind yourself that you're still alive and surviving.

# DAY 49

## Thought

Many think that acceptance brings relief from the pain. It doesn't. If anything, it hurts worse, but it does get better. Acceptance is vital to healing.

## Word

"The LORD is close to the brokenhearted and saves those who are crushed in spirit" (Psalm 34:18).

## Prayer

Lord, calm my fears and my heart. Let me not be led by my thoughts of anger or hatred. Lead me to better thoughts and emotions. Lord God, in Psalm 147:3, You said You would heal the brokenhearted and bind up their wounds. Please comfort me, Father, and give me peace and rest. Amen.

## Challenge

Many don't consider it, but sometimes reading a good, inspirational book (or even two) is a great way to meditate on your own life and where it's going, as well as how to get there. I also find writing in a journal to be very helpful.

# DAY 50

## Thought

Keep your head up. It may seem hopeless now, but with acceptance and time, the pain will soften, and you'll feel able to live again.

## Word

Death is the destiny of every man; the living should take this to heart" (Ecclesiastes 7:2).

Be still, and know that I am God. I will be exalted among the nations, I will be exalted in the earth!" (Psalm 46:10)

## Prayer

Lord, I want to become better in my thoughts and emotions. I am struggling. I want to make peace with what has happened. I know You are in control and love me, so I give all of my woes to You. Amen.

## Challenge

It's easy to become numb and unaware of the world. It hurts, but it'll keep your head clear and push you toward a better state of mind. Take moments in your day to purposely feel alive and aware. Meditation will help you to see that you are on a spiritual journey. The Lord is with us. He will help and guide us as we face the terror of owning how painful our human experience has been. The more we are able to pray, feel, and release the feelings and emotional energy, the more clearly we can tune into the emotional energy that is truth—love, light, beauty, and joy—coming from the Lord.

# Part II: Joy, Restoration

# Part II: Joy Restoration

*"I can do all things through Christ who strengthens me."*

Philippians 4:13 JUB

I decided to pursue my life's calling after a chance encounter with a major-turned-charity-organization manager. I met her while waiting for an event to start. Our mutual military experience facilitated a conversation about goals and dreams. I asked her why she changed careers, and she said it was because her husband asked her what she wanted to be remembered for. Turns out, this woman was the keynote speaker for the event and a cancer survivor. Her words left me stunned. I decided I shouldn't wait any longer to start serving the needs of others in bereavement and grief. I could no longer wait for something like a cancer diagnosis to propel me into my purpose. I needed to make each day meaningful and pursue my dreams.

As I write this book, I'm currently going through a transition of being a soldier for twenty-three years to a full-time entrepreneur, which is not easy for me. As I step out in faith and boldly proclaim what my Father has in store for me, I pray my story encourages and motivates you to move forward with confidence and the vision God has placed inside of you.

It's important to live your purpose and embrace everything you are because when you don't follow your true calling, you aren't maximizing your potential. The world is missing out on your gifts and talents. You'll feel as though you're missing out on something. Worse yet, being stuck affects your happiness, health, and relationships. It can be very painful. But when you decide to become true to yourself and live in your purpose, your life takes on a whole new meaning. You feel fulfilled, happy, and FREE.

To live in your purpose means you're living each day of your life with excitement, energy, and passion. It doesn't mean that you have to jump around screaming at the top of your lungs, unless that's your thing. Instead, you have this constant, inner voice talking to you. One that keeps you motivated and feeling giddy. Really, it's a sensation inside your soul whispering to you. It lets you know that you're on your right path in this world, and you're doing the right things to make your life better.

My goal is to guide people through the healing process, from feelings of confusion to knowing their next steps. During our coaching sessions at The Grief Helpline, I mentor them about their grief. I help them find joy, help them set goals, and encourage them to take steps to achieve their goals and dreams.

I understand what you're going through. I've been there. Asking for help is difficult. I want you to know that I'm here for you. Let me walk with you through your grief, so you heal and begin your new journey in this life. After all, you only get one life. You must make it meaningful and live each day to its fullest with faith, passion, and JOY.

To live well, you mourn well. To mourn well, you love well. To love well, you live well. You can find joy. You can be restored. You can live the Live U Imagined.

Fear stops a lot of people from moving forward. You stop reaching for your goals. But fear is nothing more than stress, anxiety, and depression. You can overcome it and succeed. This section of my book will show you how to overcome your fear. You will do this by finding support from family and friends, embracing change, and taking action, all in the hopes that you move forward in life.

# DAY 51

## Thought

Include God in the plans you make. He will act as your foundation, which will fortify your endeavors. Your plans won't fall apart because He will help you.

## Word

"Commit to the Lord whatever you do, and he will establish your plans" (Proverbs 16:3 NIV).

## Prayer

Father, let all my plans be based upon having You as their foundation. With You underlying everything I do, I cannot fall. Amen

## Challenge

Plan one small activity a day. Even small activities, like drawing, will give you a sense of accomplishment that will help motivate you toward bigger plans. Use today to draw a picture of something that means a lot to you.

# Day 52

## Thought

Obstacles may occur in your life, but you won't stumble because God is with you. He will reach out and grab you before you fall.

## Word

"The Lord will keep you from all harm he—will watch over your life" (Psalm 121:7 NIV).

## Prayer

Thank you, Father, for keeping me from falling when I stumble. Amen.

## Challenge

Write a poem expressing your feelings, how you would like to feel, or how you feel when you accomplish tasks.

# DAY 53

## Thought

You're going to have to live until your time comes. You have to get off the couch and stop feeling stuck. Start moving forward.

## Word

"Not that I have already obtained this or am already perfect, but I press on to make it my own, because Christ Jesus has made me his own"(Philippians 3:12 ESV).

## Prayer

Dear Lord, please continue to be with me as I work through everything that I am feeling. I ask that You continue to lead me back to You. Forgive me for fighting the plan You have for me, and give me the peace to accept it. Amen.

## Challenge

Consider what "start moving forward" means to you. What does it look like? Reserve fifteen minutes out of your day to be with this vision.

# DAY 54

## Thought

Blessings are a two-way street. I bless God, and I praise Him for who He is: my rock, my fortress, my loving King, my deliverer, my shield, in whom I take refuge. I acknowledge that I am nothing without Him, that I need Him, that He is the one who trains me for "war"; He rescues me. I ask boldly for Him to come down, to fight for me, to rescue and deliver me from "aliens"—those who are false and full of deceit. I ask that my family barns (bank accounts) would be full and that we would be productive, and our work would multiply; that we would be fruitful and a blessing to many, many people. All this without loss. And so I ask because my God is my Lord, and great blessings are a benefit from such a giving relationship.

## Word

"Blessed be the LORD, my rock, Who trains my hands for war, And my fingers for battle; My lovingkindness and my fortress, My stronghold and my deliverer, My shield and He in whom I take refuge, Who subdues my people under me"(Psalm 144:1–2 NASB).

## Prayer

Amazing God, You can do so much more than I can ever ask or think! Thank You that You are uncontainable, beautiful, and blessed! In Your son Jesus's name, Amen.

## Challenge

What are you believing God for? What are the dreams that He's put in your heart, for you, your children, your family, etc.? Write it down in your journal.

# DAY 55

## Thought

Obstacles—what are they to the Lord's people whom He has blessed? The advances of the enemy? The forgiving terrain was surmountable because God had given Joseph's people great power.

What are obstacles I face? Disorganization, lack of finances, lack of significant friendships, and energy. But if God is with me, all these obstacles are surmountable. Do I believe it?

## Word

"The people of Joseph said to Joshua, 'Why have you given us only one allotment and one portion for an inheritance? We are a numerous people and the LORD has blessed us abundantly'" (Joshua 17:14 NIV).

## Prayer

Oh loving and powerful God, thank You that You gave us power to overcome obstacles. Thank You that nothing is impossible with Your son. Help me to continually worship You with all my heart, soul, and mind, and protect me from the evil one as I keep believing in Your willingness and ability to bless me extravagantly. In Jesus's name, Amen.

## Challenge

What are obstacles that you face? Take on the battle by "facing the giants" in your life. The most important thing you can do is to go to God in prayer and to pray with others. Spend some time engaged in spiritual warfare. Don't let the enemy defeat you, but keep fighting by putting on the whole armor of God. And never forget that He loves you more than you can ever imagine, so much that He died for you so you could live.

# DAY 56

## Thought

My mom had lung cancer. My oldest sister had diabetes and emphysema. My brother had a massive heart attack. My second oldest sister also suffered from diabetes. The combination of different illnesses caused her heart to stop, and she had a heart attack. My youngest sister, Alicia, had diabetes. Coupled with awareness and healthy lifestyle habits, these are all diseases that can be avoided. In life we have choices, and we can make better choices for our lives by not drinking and smoking. Disease is caused by a lot of factors: foods, drugs, alcohol, stress, lack of rest, and overeating, just to name a few. At the Grief Helpline, we host workshops and classes to help with wellness issues so you can live a long and healthy life.

## Word

"Therefore, if anyone is in Christ, he is a new creation. The old has passed away; behold, the new has come" (2 Corinthians 5:17 ESV).

## Prayer

Father, give me the strength to not only lean on what I understand, but to accept the plans You have set out for me. Make me a new, more vitalized person each day. Amen.

## Challenge

Consider generational curses that may be on your family. It could be related to physical health, mental health, poor relationship choices, abuse, neglect, poverty, etc. What's the first step of alleviating these patterns in your life? Perhaps it's making an appointment to see a health professional, discovering ways that you can save more money, or assessing the influence of the company you keep. Write this down.

# Day 57

## Thought

Let us pray about anything and everything. The answer is in the prayer. Whatever you are going through, know that God will see you through it, but you have to walk and talk to the Master. He is waiting to hear from you today. Let your request be made known to him.

Remember the crisis you had to endure and the trauma you suffered—you know, the one that you were sure you would not live through or be able to overcome. You made it, which means you are a conqueror. Your power comes from His Spirit; find it inside you, grow in it, and live in it. Be filled with the Holy Spirit and let it guide you and fill your soul with love.

## Word

"For the Spirit God gave us does not make us timid, but gives us power, love and self-discipline" (2 Timothy 1:7 NIV).

## Prayer

Father, let me seek Your Spirit that lies within and learn to grow with it and in it. Let Your Spirit guide me to become the person You want me to be. Amen.

## Challenge

Search out an accountability partner. This could be a friend, family member, church member, or counselor. Sometimes an accountability partner can be the final push you need in a day of fighting temptation.

# Day 58

## Thought

If death teaches us nothing else, it makes it clear that life is too short. Live your dreams now and stop putting stuff on hold.

## Word

"Since you are my rock and my fortress, for the sake of your name lead and guide me" (Psalm 31:3).

## Prayer

Father, I have survived trauma's heartbreak and devastation, and I am still here, thanks to You, Lord God. Lord, teach me to live life to the fullest. Teach me how to live a joy-filled life all in Your name. Amen.

## Challenge

Go try something new. You've wanted to try rock climbing. Go try it! Go do something you have wanted to try, but have never gone and done! What is it that you have been wanting to do, that one thing that you had in the back of your mind. Take the leap of faith. God has your back.

# Day 59

## Thought

You're not alone. God will keep you and hold you through it all. The Lord is constantly looking over you and keeping your spirit from harm.

## Word

"The LORD will keep you from all harm—he will watch over your life; the LORD will watch over your coming and going both now and forever more" (Psalm 121:7-8).

## Prayer

Lord, hold me against You as I experience new life, new experiences, and new people. Keep me safe, calm, and near You. Amen.

## Challenge

Meditate on the Lord's love for you. Imagine His loving arms surrounding you and protecting you, because He is there.

# Day 60

## Thought

While the Lord holds us close, we must also meet him halfway. Don't live your life in a style that doesn't include God. Living a life of excess and unwise choices will lead you away from the path of God.

## Word

"Be very careful, then, how you live—not as unwise but as wise, making the most of every opportunity, because the days are evil" (Ephesians 5:15–16).

## Prayer

Father, be with me in all that I do. Hold me close to You that I may not fall into a life of sin that would only lead me farther away from You. When tempting thoughts of sinful ways try to creep into my mind, banish those thoughts, and make my mind pure again with thoughts of You, and Your great love for me. Amen.

## Challenge

Keep a journal of the good in your life. Try to associate how those good events and ongoing relationships with good and pure thoughts. Encourage yourself to live a pure life. Read the Bible and about all of God's victories this will help you to stay focused.

 143

# Day 61

## Thought

If you search out righteousness and love, you will find the good in your life that you long for. Not only look for these qualities in other people, but also attempt to make these qualities a part of your own personality.

## Word

"Whoever pursues righteousness and love finds life, prosperity and honor" (Proverbs 21:21).

## Prayer

Father, show me what true righteousness is. Don't allow my heart to confuse judgment or ill contempt for what is pure and righteous. Don't allow me to fall into hypocrisy or pride, but rather love those around me for who they are. Amen.

## Challenge

Do something for someone you don't know. Go buy a meal for the homeless man down the street, or even better, prepare him a meal. Volunteer at a women's shelter. There are so many things you can do for those that are less fortunate. Giving your time and service is planting and sowing in that you will reap a harvest if one continues to do good deeds and plant good seeds.

# DAY 62

## Thought

While the Bible calls for us to be obedient, remember that our true Master, Lord, and Savior is Christ himself. Serve the Lord, and all other things will fall into place the way God intends.

## Word

"Whatever you do, work at it with all your heart, as working for the Lord, not for human masters, since you know that you will receive an inheritance from the Lord as a reward. It is the Lord Christ you are serving" (Colossians 3:23–24).

## Prayer

Father, give me the strength to follow You and to serve You, even when it's not convenient or what I want to do. Remind me daily that I owe my entire life and being to You. Amen.

## Challenge

Sit down with your Bible. See how many passages you can find on your own where it speaks of serving the Lord. Let these scriptures be a reminder of your loyalty to God.

# Day 63

## Thought

Continuing to lean on Christ instead of ourselves can only strengthen us. We must use God as a rock and shield. If you need an answer, try God. If you need a breakthrough, try God. There is nothing he can't do.

## Word

"The Lord is my rock, my fortress, and my deliverer; my God is my rock, in whom I take refuge, my shield and the horn of my salvation, and my stronghold" (Psalm 18:2).

## Prayer

Lord, thank You for always being my rock, even when I don't deserve it. I humbly ask, please remain at my side. My life and joy depends on You, and I will not trade You, my faithful foundation, for a foundation made of sinking sand. Amen.

## Challenge

(This is especially good to do with kids). Build, or have your kid(s) build, a clay house. Pile up some sand and try to place the house on the sand pile. Give the container a good shake. Does the house stay up? Now, do the same with a stone. Does the house fall? This is a good reminder that we must build our faith and lives on Jesus, and not on the shaky things of this world.

# DAY 64

## Thought

Be thankful for what you have and live humbly. Owning everything in this world won't make you happy.

## Word

"What good is it for someone to gain the whole world, yet forfeit their soul?" (Mark 8:36)

## Prayer

Father, teach me to be humble, thankful, and joyful in the things that I am blessed with. Remind me daily that they're truly Your possessions, and to be happy with what I am allowed to have. Amen.

## Challenge

Go through your clothes, shoes, board games, and books. Donate what you don't use or need to shelters and other organizations that give such items to those who are not fortunate enough to own them.

# Day 65

## Thought

Many times we're pulled toward the ways of the world. It's okay to be in the world, but don't become a product of it. Avoid being swayed into a path less righteous than that of the path the Lord has set out for you.

## Word

"Show me your ways, Lord, teach me your paths" (Psalm 25:4).

## Prayer

Father, I ask that You remind me daily that I am here to follow Your path for me. Keep my mind and eyes from that which would defile your name. Keep me on the path that I am supposed to be on during this walk through life. Amen.

## Challenge

Write out a plan for following righteous paths and avoiding things that cause you pain, spiritually and physically. Collect a list of things to avoid and things to pursue. Write them down in your journal.

# DAY 66

## Thought

We're promised an eternal life with God after this life. What do you have to fear in death? Live life without the fear of death and what comes later. Don't be self-destructive, but live life to the absolute fullest without fear of tomorrow or what it holds. This is freeing and allows you to focus on God rather than your future troubles and concerns.

## Word

"The Lord is close to the brokenhearted and saves those who are crushed in spirit" (Psalms 34:18).

## Prayer

Lord, thank You. You have come to my rescue so many times in my life. You lifted me out of the pit and placed my feet on solid ground. You are faithful to restore lives no matter how desperate situations may be. I know that You have me in Your arms and that in the end, I will be with You in heaven. You are my hope and strength, oh Lord, my redeemer. Amen.

## Challenge

Write down all of your troubles and worries. Pray about each one, and as you do, scratch out each one so that you no longer read it. Don't worry about it anymore. You've given it to God. Let him take care of it.

"Those who joyfully leave everything in God's hand will eventually see God's hand in everything." –Nishan Panwar

# DAY 67

## Thought

Those who only pursue evil will only find evil. They won't achieve true happiness. In order to achieve true happiness, one must seek good and do good, giving their life to the Lord.

## Word

"For, Whoever would love life and see good days must keep their tongue from evil and their lips from deceitful speech. They must turn from evil and do good; they must seek peace and pursue it"(1 Peter 3:10–11).

## Prayer

Father, I need Your help to stay pure and pursue good. Give me the strength to stay away from those who promote evil and would sway me into evil. Hold me and protect me. Amen.

## Challenge

Make a list of events in your neighborhood that are working toward good and pure ends. Become involved in making your neighborhood a better place for all, especially because younger generations need guidance.

# Day 68

## Thought

When we see people who succeed in doing evil, it's very easy to question God's motives. It becomes easy to ask, "Why did you allow that to happen, God?" Remember that it's not our place to question or blame God. It's hard, but we must not worry when people succeed in evil deeds.

## Word

"Be still before the LORD and wait patiently for him; do not fret when people succeed in their ways, when they carry out their wicked schemes" (Psalm 37:7**).**

## Prayer

Lord, I see the evil in this world, and sometimes I want to ask why it is allowed. Sometimes it makes me question the world and why things happen. It sometimes makes me angry and frustrated. Please calm my worries and remind me that You are in control, not me. Sometimes things happen that I will not understand, and that is okay because You are in control. Amen.

## Challenge

Go ride a rollercoaster, let someone drive you around a place you don't know, or find another activity where you don't have complete control of the situation. Learn to trust that God will protect you, and that everything He allows to happen, happens for a reason.

# DAY 69

## Thought

Beware the "way of the sway." Many people attempt to do good and reach out to those who are not following Christ. While this is good, beware being swayed into doing the evil that you'll find when searching out those who don't follow Christ.

## Word

"Do not conform to the pattern of this world, but be transformed by the renewing of your mind. Then you will be able to test and approve what God's will is—his good, pleasing and perfect will" (Romans 12:2).

## Prayer

Father, I want to find those who don't know You. I want to gain their trust and lead them to You. However, I will face temptations. Please keep my mind pure and keep me from falling into these temptations. Amen.

## Challenge

Sign up for a program that will match you with someone struggling through life, such as the big/little sibling programs. These are good ways to reach out to those who need help and could use leading toward God.

 154

# Day 70

## Thought

God's goodness and love is always within prayer's reach. We often fi nd ourselves feeling alone, scared, and depressed. It's easy to forget that Christ promised to never leave us when we are going through diffi cult times. Remember that He follows us through it all.

## Word

"Surely your goodness and love will follow me all the days of my life, and I will dwell in the house of the LORD forever" (Psalm 23:6).

## Prayer

Lord, when I'm going through truly diffi cult things, I sometimes lose sight of You, but I know that You never lose sight of me. Thank you for continuing to carry me and keep me protected under Your wings. Amen.

## Challenge

Put a few Post-It Notes around the house reminding you that God is with you throughout all of your day. Put some at your workstation or in your lunch box for work. Put one in the car. Remind yourself to pray to God and ask for the peace that passes all understanding. We host vision board parties at our retreats. The Bible tells us, "Where *there is* no vision, the people perish" (Psalms 29:18 KJV). Another verse states, "Write down the revelation and make it plain on tablets so that a herald may run with it" (Habakkuk 2:2 NIV).

# DAY 71

## Thought

Keep your eyes on Christ. Remember to go to Him and read the word. It'll keep you spiritually fed. If you start to feel yourself needing more Christ in your life, remember that going back to the word and meditating on Him are good ways to feed your spiritual needs.

## Word

"Then Jesus declared, 'I am the bread of life. Whoever comes to me will never go hungry, and whoever believes in me will never be thirsty'"(John 6:35).

## Prayer

Father, please keep me spiritually fed. Keep me coming to You and loving You. When I feel myself slipping into despair, remind me that Your scripture is there to feed my soul and keep me near You. Amen.

## Challenge

Search out scriptures that are food for both thought and soul. Keep these scriptures as reminders of Christ's love for you.

# DAY 72

## Thought

Many see holiness as being proud or better than others, but this is not what God calls us to be. God calls us to live in peace with everyone we come in contact with. Being holy and being hypocritical are two different things, and we must strive to not fall into the temptation of being "holier than thou."

## Word

"Make every effort to live in peace with everyone and to be holy; without holiness no one will see the Lord" (Hebrews 12:14).

## Prayer

Lord, I see the way that many people act in the world, and it becomes very easy to believe that I am somehow better than them and deserve better than them. Remind me that I am a sinner as well and that we are all in debt to You. Amen.

## Challenge

Try to make amends with one person. If you can't become friends, at least become peaceful toward each other. If they don't reciprocate those feelings, then at least you have done what God calls you to do, which is making the effort toward peace.

 158

# Day 73

## Thought

God calls us to share Him with others. It's when we truly believe in Christ and all that He has to offer us that we open ourselves up to being used by Him to reach others.

## Word

"Whoever believes in me, as Scripture has said, rivers of living water will flow from within them" (John 7:38).

## Prayer

Christ, use me in whatever way You see fit to reach others and bring them to Your truth and love. I want to be an overflowing river of Your love, so that I may show the world what You have done for me and what You can do for them. Amen.

## Challenge

Find someone to witness to, even if it's a child. Tell them of the good things that have been brought to you since accepting Christ.

# DAY 74

## Thought

God will bless your obedience to Him. We may not see the benefits in this life, but we will be rewarded for following Him and His laws.

## Word

"For I command you today to love the LORD your God, to walk in obedience to him, and to keep his commands, decrees and laws; then you will live and increase, and the LORD your God will bless you in the land you are entering to possess" (Deuteronomy 30:16).

## Prayer

Father, keep me and hold me. I wish to only follow You and love You. Bless me as I walk through life for You. In Your name, Amen.

## Challenge

Pick one commandment a day to truly reflect on. If you find that you're doing things that break that commandment, work toward eliminating these temptations and sins.

# Day 75

## Thought

My mother used to tell me, "Words are like toothpaste. Once you speak words, you cannot put them back, just like you can't put toothpaste back in the tube. It's only going to make for a very messy circumstance." She was right.

## Word

"Those who guard their lips preserve their lives, but those who speak rashly will come to ruin" (Proverbs 13:3).

## Prayer

Lord, my tongue often gets in the way of teaching and following You. My mouth is that of a sinner, so I ask that You cleanse it and make it whole. Let my mouth only speak to the testimony of You. Amen.

## Challenge

(Another good one to do with kids). Buy a small tube of toothpaste. Have a child squeeze out a good amount of toothpaste. Now have them try to put it back into the bottle. When it will not go back in, explain how this relates to the things we say to others and how we should guard our thoughts and words.

# Day 76

**Thought**

Continue to study and learn all you can. Even God calls us to continue our search for knowledge, wisdom, and understanding.

**Word**

"The one who gets wisdom loves life; the one who cherishes understanding will soon prosper" (Proverbs 19:8).

**Prayer**

Lord, show me the difference in what is true and what is false as I venture to learn more about the word, the scripture, and You. Amen.

**Challenge**

Find a local class at your church or another church nearby. Create a group if you can't find a class. Learn from those around you as you study.

# Day 77

## Thought

It's often said that those who have the greatest wisdom and understanding are also the most loving and do the most for humanity. Gandhi is an example of wisdom turning into peace and insight.

## Word

"Who is wise and understanding among you? Let them show it by their good life, by deeds done in the humility that comes from wisdom" (James 3:13).

## Prayer

Lord, I ask for wisdom and understanding. Show me the true wisdom of my life, so that I may share it and do good deeds. In Your name, Amen.

## Challenge

Use what you learn from your own studies and from the studies of others to further your knowledge, and therefore, your good deeds for others.

# DAY 78

## Thought

God doesn't ask us to be great martyrs in order to accept Him as our Savior or for Him to live inside of us. Many times we find ourselves becoming wrapped up in the services God asks us to perform that we believe good deeds are how we find Him, but this isn't what God has told us.

## Word

"If anyone acknowledges that Jesus is the Son of God, God lives in them and they in God" (1 John 4:15).

## Prayer

Lord, I love You. I accept You, and I acknowledge that Your Son is Jesus Christ. It brings me great joy to know that He lives within me, and I within Him. Amen.

## Challenge

Meditate on what it means to have Christ living within you.

# Day 79

## Thought

God doesn't want you to dwell on the past. He wants you to focus on the present and look to the future. You must let go of what's holding you back. Release your mistakes and misfortunes. Move forward with renewed hope and walk into the journey to joy.

## Word

"But I would not have you to be ignorant, brethren, concerning them which are asleep, that ye sorrow not, even as others which have no hope. For if we believe that Jesus died and rose again, even so them also which sleep in Jesus will God bring with him" (1 Thessalonians 4:13–14).

## Prayer

Father, it's time for me to forget the past, forget the mistakes, and focus on what you are doing in my life today. I know you are doing a new thing in my life and removing the wrong ones. You are closing old doors and preparing me for new opportunities. The pruning process can be uncomfortable and painful, but I know it's for my good. I trust you. In Jesus's name, Amen.

## Challenge

As you awake and stand at the beginning of a new day, create a vision to see the best is yet to come. Use your wisdom to make good decisions, and most of all, walk in the faith that you are walking with Jesus every step of the way.

# Day 80

## Thought

As a young and sometimes rebellious teenager, I often found my mother not allowing me to associate with certain people. "They're not that bad," I thought at the time, but she had good reasons to not allow such friendships. Sometimes you have to say goodbye to good and hello to *great*.

## Word

"Whoever heeds discipline shows the way to life, but whoever ignores correction leads others astray"(Proverbs 10:17).

## Prayer

Father, it's easy to ignore discipline and correction. Especially as adults, we don't believe that we need to be corrected. Please continue to remind me that I do need Your leadership, so that I may lead others to You. Amen.

## Challenge

Find a project online. Follow the instructions to the letter. Although this seems simple, many find they have trouble following directions and instead want to plow forward on their own.

# Day 81

## Thought

Did you know that when you give yourself to the Lord, you are dying and becoming a new life?

## Word

"I have been crucified with Christ and I no longer live, but Christ lives in me. The life I now live in the body, I live by faith in the Son of God, who loved me and gave himself for me" (Galatians 2:20).

## Prayer

Father, it's easy to fall back into the same bad habits. I ask that You remind me that this is no longer my life but Yours. My life belongs to You, and I should use it for Your will, not my own. Amen.

## Challenge

When you find yourself doing something that is only beneficial to yourself, ask what God would have you do in the situation instead if He were sitting right beside you.

# DAY 82

## Thought

God went through the ultimate pain, so that we may have joy.

## Word

"This is how God showed his love among us: He sent his one and only Son into the world that we might live through him"(1 John 4:9).

## Prayer

Father, I cannot imagine the pain You suffered when you gave Your only Son, so that we may live our lives free of the payment for sin. Thank You for making the ultimate sacrifice for me. Amen.

## Challenge

You have to know that you are enough. That God has placed everything you need on the inside of you. Today is a good day to listen to your Soaking music.

# DAY 83

## Thought

It's easy to want to believe in only what we see, but to have true happiness, we must live by faith. Imagine for a second that there was no wind. The world would be completely different. We wouldn't be able to cool ourselves off. Clouds wouldn't move to bring shade or rain. However, we cannot see the wind, and yet it brings us so much joy. The Lord works in much the same way.

## Word

"For we live by faith, not by sight"(2 Corinthians 5:7).

## Prayer

Father, I find myself losing sight of You. It becomes hard sometimes when I cannot see You directly in front of me. Please continue to strengthen my faith. Amen.

## Challenge

Go outside and feel the wind across your face. We cannot see the wind, but we can certainly feel and see the effects of the wind. He brings us joy.

# DAY 84

## Thought

My mother used to say to me, "If you would simply follow my instructions, you'd be a lot happier." It wasn't until I was much older that I began to understand what she meant. Rules are there to keep us safe, much like the commandments in the Bible.

## Word

"He replied, 'Blessed, rather are those who hear the word of God and obey it'"(Luke 11:28).

## Prayer

Father, I know I don't always obey. Please forgive me where I fail and help me to do better next time. Teach me Your word, so I may follow it closely. Amen.

## Challenge

Make yourself more familiar with the commandments of God's word. Study scripture that offers insight into how God wants us to act.

# Day 85

## Thought

Looking back on the past won't bring you happiness in the present. Much like the man who looked back at what he had plowed so far, only to mess up what he was plowing at the time, you too will only make yourself more miserable by searching the past.

## Word

"Do not say, 'Why were the old days better than these?' For it is not wise to ask such questions" (Ecclesiastes 7:10).

## Prayer

Father, keep my eyes on You and the present joys You have provided. I don't want to become old, angry, and bitter. I want to be happy in the present and not burden myself with things of the past. Amen.

## Challenge

Move forward and try new things. Get a haircut, eat that hefty bowl of ice cream, or do something out of the norm. Live in the now.

# Day 86

## Thought

My mother had many old tales and wise words to live by. One thing she used to always say was to not let your heart turn bitter or dark. She would say that the heart is where our love for others comes from, so if we let it become full of hate, hate is what we will show and give others.

## Word

"Above all else, guard your heart, for everything you do flows from it" (Proverbs 4:23).

## Prayer

Father, there are times that this world gets me down, angry, and depressed. It's in these times that I want to lash out and become hurtful to others. Please don't allow such darkness to enter my heart or tarnish Your name. Amen.

## Challenge

Go to someone who has done you wrong. Tell them you forgive them and really mean it. Letting go of this hate will give you more joy than you can imagine.

# DAY 87

## Thought

God calls us to be His witnesses. Once we hand our lives over to Him, they are His, and we will find happiness in spreading the good news of Christ's gift to us.

## Word

"However, I consider my life worth nothing to me; my only aim is to finish the race and complete the task the Lord Jesus has given me—the task of testifying to the good news of God's grace" (Acts 20:24).

## Prayer

Lord, I have been set on this path to do Your will. I know that my joy will come from following Your will, and I thank You for such an opportunity. Amen.

## Challenge

Take an evangelizing class. Learn how to more readily and easily share the Lord's word. God put you in this race, so live it!

# Day 88

## Thought

Throughout our lives we are told that worrying won't settle anything. It'll only make things worse. It turns out that the Bible preaches the exact same advice. Will you heed it?

## Word

"Therefore I tell you, do not worry about your life, what you will eat or drink; or about your body, what you will wear. Is not life more than food, and the body more than clothes?" (Matthew 6:25)

## Prayer

Lord, while I find it hard to let go of my troubles and worries, I know that You have me in Your arms. Please help me to let You have it all and not hold onto what is troubling my heart. Amen.

## Challenge

Write a song that tells God all about your troubles and giving them to Him. Let Him have your worries. What do you need them for?

# DAY 89

## Thought

This is the day that the Lord has made! Who are we to walk around in it grumbling or mad? No, instead we should rejoice and be glad for the day we're given!

## Word

"The LORD has done it this very day; let us rejoice today and be glad" (Psalm 118:24).

## Prayer

Heavenly Father, how I thank You for the great joy that You give me each day. Thank You for Jesus and the joy and peace that floods the hearts of all who accept Him. Amen.

## Challenge

Go out and smell the flowers. No, really. Go smell the flowers. It's raining? Awesome! Go feel the cool rain on your face. God has made this day for you. Rejoice in its gifts!

# Day 90

## Thought

Some days it seems impossible to be joyful about the world. Sometimes we face trials and tribulations beyond our pain threshold. It's days like these that we must persevere and trust in the Lord.

## Word

"Blessed is the one who perseveres under trial because, having stood the test, that person will receive the crown of life that the Lord has promised to those who love him" (James 1:12).

## Prayer

Lord, today is especially difficult. There are a lot of events happening in my life right now that I don't understand and that cause me pain. Please see me through these trials, as I put my faith in You. Amen.

## Challenge

Meditate on the things that are causing you trouble in your life right now. Concentrate on giving them a physical form in your mind, and then, mentally and spiritually hand them over to God.

# Day 91

## Thought

Have you given your life to the Lord? If so, then who are we to use His life to mope, be sad or depressed, or get angry? When we give our lives to the Lord, we are giving Him our all, and that includes the way we perceive the day He has given us.

## Word

"If we live, we live for the Lord; and if we die, we die for the Lord. So, whether we live or die, we belong to the Lord" (Romans 14:8).

## Prayer

Loving Father, I thank You for this time You have given me and the life I have been given. I pray that Your joy and peace would rest upon me and that I overflow with Your Holy Spirit, so that I may share Your grace with the world. Amen.

## Challenge

Imagine for the day, that your life, body, and world is controlled by God. What would He do differently throughout the day from what you would? Are these things you should strive to do with your day as well?

# DAY 92

## Thought

God has given us all the guidance we need. It's simply up to us to accept that guidance, and then, to live by it. God is a towering lighthouse for us to follow. Does your life look like a mirror of His? Or have you let your lighthouse beam burn out?

## Word

"You are the light of the world. A town built on a hill cannot be hidden"(Matthew 5:14).

## Prayer

Lord, You call me to be a mirror of You. You call me to love and to be a light unto others like You. Please give me every opportunity to be that for You and for others. Amen.

## Challenge

Find songs that speak of being a light unto others. There are many out there, and meditating on them can bring great understanding and love to your life, as well as joy.

# DAY 93

## Thought

You're worth more than you'll ever know! Be happy about that! Your life can't be bought with material items, such as money or gold. You were purchased with the very blood of Christ! What happier news is there?

## Word

"For you know that it was not with perishable things such as silver or gold that you were redeemed from the empty way of life handed down to you from your ancestors, but with the precious blood of Christ, a lamb without blemish or defect" (1 Peter 1:18–19).

## Prayer

Father, I sometimes feel that I am not worthy of life. It's then that I feel ashamed. I remember that Your Son gave His life for me, making me more worthy than all the riches in the world. Thank you for Your sacrifice. Amen.

## Challenge

Write a thank you letter to God. Tell Him all you're thankful for in your life.

# Day 94

## Thought

Anger is one of the greatest sources of despair, rather than love and joy. This is why God calls us not to become angry too quickly and to not wage a war against others.

## Word

"For though we live in the world, we do not wage war as the world does" (2 Corinthians 10:3).

## Prayer

Lord, forgive me. I have become angry and have wanted harm to come to someone else. Forgive me, as I forgive them. Amen.

## Challenge

Make a list of those who have wronged you that you hold anger toward. Each day, pray for one person and pray for your own forgiveness of that person.

# DAY 95

## Thought

The Lord can see all that has ever been, all that is, and all that will ever be. With that, our tiny time on earth seems short and insignificant, but even so, the Lord chooses to keep and watch over each of us. Rejoice in this fact.

## Word

"A thousand years in your sight are like a day that has just gone by, or like a watch in the night" (Psalm 90:4).

## Prayer

Father, in a world where there are so many difficult situations, troubled times, and hurting hearts, I ask that You remember me. Hold me, protect me, and love me, and I will rejoice in this. Amen.

## Challenge

Look for church festivals, plays, or films. Enjoy the entertainment, but also meditate in how God looks out for each of His followers that work to share Him and His word.

# DAY 96

## Thought

God calls us to be great witnesses amongst the people we're surrounded by. How can we expect to be great witnesses if we allow sadness or anger to overcome our lives?

## Word

"Therefore, since we are surrounded by such a great cloud of witnesses, let us throw off everything that hinders and the sin that so easily entangles. And let us run with perseverance the race marked out for us"(Hebrews 12:1).

## Prayer

Lord, I know my testimony and the way I live affects those around me. I want to bring more people to You, not turn them away, so please let them see the joy You bring me each day and not the faults of my own human sins. Amen.

## Challenge

Write out your testimony. Share your testimony with someone who's struggling or looking for Christ.

# DAY 97

## Thought

You have nothing to fear. The Lord protects those who serve Him, and you'll forever be with Him. One of my favorite reminders of God's love and power comes from the children's program *Veggie Tales*. The line goes,, "God is bigger than the Boogie Man, and He's watching out for you and me."

## Word

"The LORD will rescue his servants; no one who takes refuge in him will be condemned" (Psalm 34:22).

## Prayer

Father, Your plan is always best. Sometimes the process is painful and hard. Trust in God's timing. It's better to wait awhile and have things fall into place than to rush and have things fall apart. Remember, wait on God. When he is done, everything will be better. Amen.

## Action

Watch the *Veggie Tales* episode, "Where's God When I'm Scared?" Seriously, it's a good watch!

# Day 98

## Thought

God set you free; don't go back to the same old sins! God gave you your freedom from those sins, so there's no reason to go back to them. They won't bring you true happiness and will only lead you away from Christ. There is a saying, "Good things come to those who believe, better things to come to those who are patient, and the best things come to those who don't give up."

## Word

"And regarding the question, friends, that has come up about what happens to those already dead and buried, we don't want you in the dark any longer. First off, you must not carry on over them like people who have nothing to look forward to, as if the grave were the last word. Since Jesus died and broke loose from the grave, God will most certainly bring back to life those who died in Jesus" (1 Thessalonians 4:13–14).

## Prayer

Lord, I find myself tempted to go back to my once wicked ways. Please steer me away from these things and keep me under Your guarded wings. Hold me in Your arms. Don't let me perish. Amen.

## Challenge

Find things to occupy your time other than the sinful things you've allowed to fill your time before.

# DAY 99

## Thought

Each day has enough worries of its own, so don't give a single day more worry than it deserves. This will only zap any joy you had for the day.

## Word

"Therefore do not worry about tomorrow, for tomorrow will worry about itself. Each day has enough trouble of its own" (Matthew 6:34).

## Prayer

Lord, I ask for the peace that surpasses all understanding. Give me the hope and joy that I know only You can deliver. Amen.

## Challenge

Make a list of things for tomorrow that'll bring you joy when you do them. When you begin to think of things that worry you, flip instead to something that's going to bring you joy.

# Day 100

## Thought

The Lord conquers all. There's nothing the Lord can't handle, so when you find yourself overwhelmed, simply look to Him for guidance.

## Word

"For this is what the high and exalted One says—he who lives forever, whose name is holy: "I live in a high and holy place, but also with the one who is contrite and lowly in spirit, to revive the spirit of the lowly and to revive the heart of the contrite"(Isaiah 57:15).

## Prayer

Lord, I know You can and do take care of me. Please don't let me falter in my faith. Protect and guide me and my loved ones all the rest of my days. Amen.

## Challenge

"Whenever you find yourself doubting how far you can go, just remember how far you have come. Remember everything you have faced, all the battles you have won, and all the fears you have overcome." —Unknown

Sit in a quiet room and let your mind wander. Think about all of the good things God has done for you. Let the joy those things bring fill you up to the very brim. Take that joy with you as you go out into the world and face your daily demons. God is not blind, and He is not deaf. Every tear you have cried, every prayer you have prayed, and every obstacle you face, is not being overlooked. Trust God. He is not going to leave you. He won't allow his children to lose anything that he can't restore.

# Epilogue

Tragedy is difficult. Eventually, we must move on, but that's not always easy to do. It certainly wasn't for me, but I understand that the family members I've lost are in a better place now, and I know that one day I'm going to see them again. I also know that one day I'll pass on too, and just as I want my loved ones to keep moving forward, I'm sure they'd want the same thing for me.

Helping you to spring back into action after loss is extremely important to me. I want you to be able to thank God for the good memories while continuing to make many more good memories on your journey to joy!

If you take away nothing else from this experience, I want to you remember two verses:

1. "For everything there is a season, and a time for every matter under heaven: a time to be born, and a time to die; a time to plant, and a time to pluck up what is planted; a time to kill, and a time to heal; a time to break down, and a time to build up; a time to weep, and a time to laugh; a time to mourn, and a time to dance; a time to cast away stones, and a time to gather stones together" (Ecclesiastes 3:1–5 ESV).

This is true for grief recovery. Sadness and sorrow are a part of the human experience. While difficult, these must be accepted. They also must be honored as gifts, for after they've come, it becomes a time of growth and new beginnings.

2.  "Your Sorrow will be turned into joy" (John 16:20).

    This is true for joy restoration. In order to live in your purpose, you must move forward with confidence and with the vision God has placed inside of you.

Creating a plan for your life after loss is essential, and you have to take steps every single day to make those plans a reality. Even if it's a baby step, action is action. If you aren't following your true calling, then you aren't maximizing your potential. The world is missing out on your gifts and talents. Being stuck like this affects your happiness, health, and relationships, and that can be very painful. But when you decide to become true to yourself and live in your purpose, your life takes on a whole new meaning.

# ABOUT THE AUTHOR

Vernessa Blackwell is a veteran, author, and certified grief support and joy restoration coach. She earned her masters in business administration at Strayer University, and during her twenty-four-year career in the military, she served in numerous positions in the human resource arena. The loss of both parents and all her siblings, to include three sisters and a brother, sparked her purposeful journey into coaching.

Her heartfelt mission is to enrich, inspire, and uplift after loss to help you honor and remember the beautiful life of someone you care about.

Vernessa has co-authored several books, including *Camouflaged Sisters*, *Activate: 24 Laws to Thrive to Win*, *Head Ladies in Charge*, *You Are Beautiful*, *Daily Decisions for Mothers*, and *Spiritual Disciplines*. She currently lives in Waldorf, Maryland. When she is not busy guiding clients through grief, she can be found traveling, reading, and spending time with her daughters, Darkema and Takia, and her seven grandchildren: Tyquan, Kemonte, Khyeema, Davonte, Khalil, Terrence Jr., and Kamille.

Vernessa believes that you should not wait for a life-shattering moment to propel you into your purpose, so contact her today at www.GriefHelpline.coach or (240) 270-1522.

**Learn more about Vernessa at:**

www.VernessaBlackwell.com
www.GriefHelpline.coach

| | |
|---|---|
| Facebook: | Vernessa.Blackwell |
| Twitter: | @GriefCoach |
| Periscope: | @GriefCoach |
| Instagram: | @GriefCoach |

# SHARE YOUR THOUGHTS

**With the Author:** If this book has impacted you in any way, the author would be delighted to hear about it. Send an email to *author@publishyourgift.com*.

**Looking for a Speaker?** Book the author to speak at your next event by writing to *booking@publishyourgift.com*.

Discover great books, exclusive offers, and more at
**www.PublishYourGift.com**

Connect with us on social media

@publishyourgift

# References

1. Karla Downing, "Getting Past Stage One – Denial," Ezine Articles, July 26, 2001, http://ezinearticles.com/?Getting-Past-Stage-One---Denial&id=6453199.

2. Karla Downing, "Christian Relationship Devotional: Letting Go of Denial," Change My Relationship, 2013, http://www.changemyrelationship.com/christian-relationship-devotional-letting-go-of-denial/.

3. Raymond T. Brock, *Handling Loss and Grief* (Cincinnati, OH: Turning Point, 1996).

4. Brenda Stroth, "Unceasing Prayer," BrendaStroth.com, June 23, 2015, http://brendastroth.com/2015/06/23/unceasing-prayer/.

5. Elisabeth Kubler-Ross and David Kessler, *On Grief and Grieving: Finding the Meaning of Grief through the Five Stages of Loss* (New York: Scribner, 2014).

6. Julie Axelrod, "The 5 Stages of Loss and Grief," Psych Central, accessed on May 2, 2016, http://psychcentral.com/lib/the-5-stages-of-loss-and-grief/.

# SOURCES

9 781945 558078